BECOMING THE
EXPRESSION
OF THE
FATHER

The Place Where His Desires Become Yours

Charles A. Haun

BECOMING THE EXPRESSION OF THE FATHER: The Place Where His Desires Become Yours

Teaching All Nations
705 Milan Ct.
Altamonte Springs, FL 32714

ISBN 0-924748-31-1
Printed in the United States of America
© 2004 by Violet Haun

Milestones International Publishers
4410 University Dr., Ste. 113
Huntsville, AL 35816
Ph: 256-536-9402 ext. 234   Fax: 256-536-4530
www.milestonesinternationalpublishers.com

Cover design by: Kirk Douponce/DogEaredDesign

1 2 3 4 5 6 7 8 9 10 11 / 10 09 08 07 06 05 04

CONTENTS

iii

A NOTE FROM
THE PUBLISHER

I knew Charles Haun, and his life had a great impact on mine. Although Charles has already gone on to be with the Lord, his teachings and messages contain such valuable experience and wisdom that it seemed important to make them available to people today. In fact, as I began reviewing the material for this book, the timeless challenge of loving God above self and all else once again seemed to be attainable. Could I meet that challenge? Could I become so close to God as to express His character to those around me? The timeless teachings of Charles Haun, as presented in this book, have once again impacted my life, and I know that they will influence your life as well.

—Jim Rill

DEDICATION

To Violet, my sweet wife

For her sacrificial love

Given as unselfishly as Christ gave His.

The love of God is shed abroad in our hearts by the Holy Ghost which is given unto us.

Romans 5:5

(From an inscription in a Bible that
Charles Haun bought for his wife.)

ACKNOWLEDGMENTS

(Throughout his life, Charles Haun acknowledged various people who incalculably contributed to his life and ministry. These individuals are mentioned here.)

Kathryn Kuhlman: Not only did I receive salvation during one of her meetings, but the word that she spoke brought light to me and showed me the value of teaching the Word of God. I was blessed to have been personally in contact with her through the years.

Walter Beuttler: A Bible teacher at Eastern Bible Institute, he added to the value of the Word and Spirit working together, which created a hunger in me to know God in all His fullness.

Wade Taylor: Founder of Pinecrest Bible Training Center, he served as a friend who was always there when I needed one and who served as a source of encouragement to me.

The family of Charles Haun also would like to acknowledge *Jim Rill*, one of Charles's students. It is his obedience to the Lord that has allowed this book to see completion.

"I've come to a point of love for my family that just time spent in the presence of Violet, the girls [Telva, Renay, Brenda, and Cindy] or grandchildren is above most joys I can have."

Charles Haun (A journal entry)

FOREWORD

The grace of God so worked in the life of Charles Haun that it brought him to a place of great trust and inward rest whereby he could truly cast all of his care upon the Lord. In that place of abiding, God brought him into spiritual maturity.

Charles was a father in the faith and, as such, expressed the heavenly Father's heart. His training ground included the jungles of Peru while a missionary to the headhunters there. It was a place of much self-denial, but he was willing to pay the price to buy the truth and sell it not, yet he would freely and eagerly share it with others.

These pages contain that truth and revelation. But they hold much more than that, for they are filled with the *spirit* of wisdom and revelation in the knowledge of Jesus Christ. Having truth and revelation is good, but having the spirit of truth and revelation is better, for the former can be the dead letter of the law while the latter is spirit and life.

As young Bible school students and little children in the faith, my fellow classmates and I would bask in that life while Charles taught. His words possessed all the characteristics of the Word of God described in the Scriptures: They were like a hammer that broke the rock of a hard heart in pieces; wheat that fed the hungry soul as opposed to empty chaff; a fire that both burned within us and consumed dross; and a sword that cut often and deep, yet brought healing to our hearts. Those same characteristics fill these pages and will fill your heart as you read.

As a father, Charles loved his children with the same care he had received from the Lord. His heart was intertwined with their spiritual progress and success. Joy or sorrow—children can be the source of either to a loving father.

The apostle Paul expressed a father's sorrow and concern when he said, *"My little children, of whom I travail in birth again until Christ be formed in you"* (Galatians 4:19). Paul's life was poured out on their behalf.

John the Beloved, also a father in the faith, declared, *"I have no greater joy than to hear that my children walk in truth"* (3 John 4). So too did Charles find his satisfaction and delight in those who heard the word of the Spirit and became conformed to it. Children do not always understand the love and care of a father toward them. Oftentimes a father is misjudged. But as a child grows into maturity, he comes into an ever greater appreciation for the father's heart toward him.

As I write this, my heart and mind are filled with appreciation for the price Charles paid to bring spirit and life. A man of God—that is, a man who comes in the name of the Lord—brings true prosperity to many needy souls. (See Psalm 118:25-26.) As he faithfully followed the will of God for his life, Charles was made broken bread and poured out wine for the body of Christ. And now that love is expressed in these pages. The table is spread, and out from his heart, the Father calls, "Come and dine."

Jacob Luffy

INTRODUCTION

The Christian life is not so much about the hows and wherefores of living righteously on earth as it is about first realizing who God is and then proceeding to love Him so much that His desires suddenly become your own. When you become acquainted with the heart of God by living so close to Him that you actually begin to feel His heartbeat, then it is not difficult to become the expression of His love to others around you. Without that, your attempt to love will be a struggle that you will ultimately lose.

For years now, we have labored to find just the right techniques for serving God, but it is not about techniques. It is about a person, the person of God. When we desire to create an atmosphere where His expression can be felt and known, then He begins to work on our behalf and to reveal His power and presence with us and through us. The result is that all those with whom we come in contact know that we are His. This is true Christianity being lived out in our daily lives. This is what it means to become the expression of the Father.

These truths are of infinite value to us because as Christians we are not just trying to live an exemplary life down here and make it into heaven. We are preparing for the greater life, for a greater role that God has destined us to play in eternity. What He sees in us here will determine how much He can entrust to our care in the hereafter.

Through the years, in my experience as pastor, missionary, and Bible teacher, I encountered some truths that I felt were key to enabling me to live a successful Christian life, and I was able to teach them to others, and they, too, were successful. These are not things that come to us automatically. There are Christians, and then there are Christians who go further. They are not satisfied just to make it into heaven. They desire a higher level of intimacy with the Father. It is to these that the Father reveals Himself more, and it is these who are allowed to become expressions of Himself in the earth. I am fortunate to have become one of those.

It began very early in my Christian experience (for instance, with the miraculous healing of my brother from polio when I was still a student in Bible school) and with God speaking to me in many miraculous ways, and it continued to grow in intensity as I matured in my relationship with God. It was demonstrated in my life as a young pastor and then, even more so, in my life as a missionary to the Amazon region of Peru. There I ate contaminated food and felt no harm from it, I faced warring native Indians and troublesome boa constrictors and lived to tell about it, and I narrowly escaped death in small airplanes, from crossing raging streams, and from waking up one night to find the houseboat on which our family lived during mission trips up and down the Amazon and its tributaries loosed from its moorings and being swept along by the mighty Amazon after a storm.

And that is just the tip of the iceberg. Over a period of many years of knowing God, I have come to experience His love and grace more and more in my personal life and to see that His desires toward us are far beyond anything we have yet imagined. His will for us is so much higher than our will for ourselves that it would behoove all of us to stop a moment and turn directions, His direction. He is great, and nothing could be more important or more rewarding in life than becoming expressions of Him to those around us.

Chapter One

KNOWING GOD

By faith Moses, when he was come to years, refused to be called the son of Pharaoh's daughter; choosing rather to suffer affliction with the people of God, than to enjoy the pleasures of sin for a season; esteeming the reproach of Christ greater riches than the treasures in Egypt: for he had respect unto the recompence of the reward.

Hebrews 11:24-26

For those who desire to know God's power, there is a bit of a price to pay. It has never been popular to deviate from the common path. For those who desire to know God's presence, there is an even greater cost involved. They will surely be misunderstood and reviled. But the greatest price is reserved, or so I have come to believe, for those who want to know God's person. Being more closely identified with Him has always had its price tag in this world.

The disciples, for instance, were not sure they wanted to be identified with Jesus after He had been arrested. He was on His way to the cross, and their fear was that if they identified too closely with Him they would die also. Knowing Jesus fully requires personal loss, and, for most Christians, that is a pill they are neither ready nor willing to swallow.

If we are to identify with Jesus, we must suffer some of what He suffered. He gave everything, and the very thought of having to do that terrifies most Christians. But we must remember that when we lose all in this world, we actually gain all in Christ.

Because of the high cost involved with knowing Jesus more intimately, most people are unwilling to even attempt it. What a pity! Knowing Jesus is everything. In Him *is* everything. To know Him is to know perfection. To know Him is to know blamelessness. To know Him is to know completion. To know Him is to know life itself.

The Price Moses Paid to Know God

The writer of Hebrews used Moses as an example of someone willing to risk all to know the Lord better. If anyone ever had everything going for him in life, it was Moses. He "had it made," as we say. He was raised in Pharaoh's courts and was groomed to become a high-ranking Egyptian official, quite probably even an actual pharaoh. This may be the reason the ruling pharaoh was so angry when Moses later sided with the Hebrews.

We can only surmise what might have been Moses' if he had chosen another path. Surely he could have easily enjoyed great riches and a position of respect. And who in his right mind would want to leave that, especially in exchange for the leadership of a group of stiff-necked people wandering in the wilderness and fighting over who would be greatest if and when they finally arrived in the Promised Land? In retrospect, Moses seems to have gotten a pretty bad deal.

That is...unless you look at it from his unique perspective. If you did not know the whole story and how it ended, you might wonder about Moses' choices. But he made his choices having seen the end from the beginning and having examined all sides of the issue. He even must have had a glimpse of the glory he would ultimately experience in God's presence when it was all said and done.

There is no doubt about it: Moses made the right choice. Staying with Egypt, the most powerful and wealthy nation of its time, would have seemed the logical choice for most, but Moses had a heavenly vision. He saw beyond the storehouses of Egypt and into the storehouses of heaven.

We know this because of something very peculiar that is said here in Hebrews 11. It says that Moses esteemed *"the reproach of Christ greater riches than the treasures in Egypt."* Although Moses knew all about *"the treasures in Egypt,"* what could he possibly have known about *"the reproach of Christ"*? This necessarily speaks of the fact that Moses had revelation from God, for there can be no other explanation as to why he would have known future events. He based his personal decisions on what God had shown him would happen in the future, and that was his strength.

Our God Is the Great Disturber

There are many levels of knowing Christ, and each of us must decide to what extent we are willing to sacrifice to know Him better. Are we satisfied to know Him as Savior and Redeemer, or (as is too often the case) simply as Provider, He who supplies all our material needs? Will we invite Him into our homes and welcome Him to stay—as long as He does not disturb anything?

Oh, but He is the Great Disturber. Think of how He disturbed the Jewish leaders of His day. He was not satisfied just to meet them; He had to shine His light on the aspects of their lives that were not pleasing to God. That type of spiritual meddling is always troublesome to those who choose to live for the here and now and not for eternity. Like many, the Pharisees refused to be happy about the Lord's pointing out their shortcomings. He seemed to be forever drawing attention to errors in their theology and in their treatment of their fellow man. This habit of His threatened their authority over the people.

3

Becoming the Expression of the Father

Many times the Pharisees wished that Jesus would just go away; they even plotted ways to help Him disappear. They listened carefully to His teachings, but not with a hungry heart, eager to learn some new truth that would lead them to a better life. Their motivation was to pick everything He said apart with a fine-toothed comb, trying to find anything at all that they could use against Him. These men hated Jesus and were constantly looking for ways to put Him down.

To those who choose not to follow Him and also to those who follow Him only halfheartedly, He is definitely a Disturber. But He is also a Disturber to those who desire to go deeper. He will disturb your life too—if you allow Him to do it. And if you can live through the turbulence of the tests and trials you will face as a result of your choice to know Him better, you will be rewarded with a greater intimacy with the Creator. That should be our highest goal in life.

The writer of Hebrews recommended:

Let us go forth therefore unto him without the camp, bearing his reproach.

Hebrews 13:13

This is the secret. Bear His reproach; identify yourself with Him; and, in the process, disassociate yourself from what is currently popular. Press through the disturbance to reach the face of Jesus, and you will come to know Him in a new and more intimate way.

Paul, too, knew what it was to identify with Jesus, and he paid a great price for it as well:

But what things were gain to me, those I counted loss for Christ. Yea doubtless, and I count all things but loss for the excellency of the knowledge of Christ Jesus my Lord: for whom I have suffered the loss of all things, and do count them but dung, that I may win Christ.

Philippians 3:7-8

Paul used his testimony very forcefully to show where he had come from, where he had gone, and how he had gotten there. His testimony, therefore, is very enlightening to those who want to go deeper. We may not all walk in exactly the same footsteps as Paul did, but his testimony can serve us as a general guide. If we desire the same intimacy with the Almighty that he achieved, we must pay a similar price. This is where many people come to a point of separation.

What Paul Left Behind to Follow Christ

Paul counted *"things"* that the world considered *"gain"* (and that he also had once considered *"gain"*) as *"loss"* for Christ. No wonder he excelled in ministry, wrote more than half of the New Testament, and established the early Gentile churches. In all of this, he was not just trying to do good works to earn some points. He wanted to *"win Christ."* That is the secret. That is our desire. That is our motivation.

Paul, like Moses, had a lot going for him. His parents were wealthy and gave him a very good education. He was a citizen of the Roman Empire at a time when that status afforded many privileges. He spoke many languages and moved easily among people of many countries and cultures. He could have easily earned a very good living and enjoyed the good life. Still, he chose to count it all as *"dung"* (waste, manure) so that he could win Christ.

Some manure does have value (as fertilizer), but that value is not very great. Paul was able to see into the spirit world and to determine that what he had considered to be extremely valuable was actually of little value, and vice versa. This enabled him to make the right choices in life.

We tend to put a monetary value on everything these days, and that somehow helps us to compare things and weigh their worth. With our businesses and our homes, for example, we assign values that help us to understand where we stand financially and if we are making any progress, or if we have anything worth protecting and improving. This is exactly what Paul did in the spirit world, and he decided that much of what had seemed valuable to him in the past was little more than *"dung"* (in the light of eternity), and he decided to let it all go (if necessary) to gain Christ.

I am not suggesting that it is wrong to have possessions, and Paul did not teach that either. But it is certainly wrong to allow possessions to control us (a subject that we will explore in more detail later). Paul needed certain things for his travels and sometimes wrote to his companions requesting specific items, but he refused to allow anything to take control of his life and unduly influence his decisions.

We need to ask ourselves if the kind of car we drive will make any difference in eternity or if the material used on the floor of our living rooms will make any difference there. In my years in ministry, I have preached in beautiful mansions, and I have preached in some of the humblest shacks in the world. In the Amazon, we lived among people who had no floors at all (or just dirt floors) in their homes. But they, too, came to know Christ and to enjoy the riches of His love. It is all relative, and we need to get our priorities straight.

Young Christians especially (but also Christians of all ages) are much too susceptible to the lure of nice things. We must become willing to lay aside anything at all to gain Christ.

The finest automobile eventually wears out, rusts out, or is wrecked and becomes little more than a pile of junk. As beautiful and as useful as nice things can be, do not allow any of them to keep you from the Pearl of Great Price—Jesus.

None of us minds comfort, and, given the choice, most of us opt for comfortable things, comfortable surroundings, and as many conveniences as possible. There is nothing wrong with that. But our focus must be on gaining Christ, on knowing Him—and nothing else.

I know what it is to wear a $35 suit, and I know what it is to wear a $500 suit. The $500 suit is definitely nicer, but I would not allow one to interfere with my spiritual life for any reason whatsoever. Paul knew both extremes of earthly prosperity, and he learned to live with both and to be content (see Philippians 4:11-13, a text we will explore in more detail and in a slightly different context later on).

Develop the right attitude about things, and they will never hinder your quest for Christ. Know His value, and things will suddenly be returned to their proper perspective.

In general, most things do not last long. They quickly go out of style. They break. They otherwise deteriorate. Count them as worthless in relationship to your desire for Christ, and you will never have a problem with them. Let things serve you while you serve God. That is where the true value in life is.

Paul went even further:

> ...that I may win Christ, and be found in him, not having mine own righteousness, which is of the law, but that which is through the faith of Christ, the righteousness which is of God by faith: that I may know him, and the power of his resurrection, and the fellowship of his sufferings, being made conformable unto his death.
>
> Philippians 3:8-10

Does this suggest that Paul did not know Christ at the time he wrote these words? Of course not. If Paul did not know Christ, then no man can know Him. By the time he wrote these words, Paul was already an older man with many remarkable accomplishments to his name. He was a respected apostle and leader of the church. Oh, he knew Christ all right.

So, when Paul says, *"that I may win Christ,"* his words serve two purposes: one, to show us how to know Christ more intimately, and two, to indicate that with all his experience, Paul still had a burning desire to know Christ better. That is always the mark of a great Christian. We must never rest on our laurels or glory in past experiences. We must be ever pressing onward to know our Lord more fully and intimately.

Becoming the Expression of the Father

The path that Paul chose to knowing Christ more intimately was knowing *"the power of his resurrection,"* and *"the fellowship of his sufferings,"* and *"being made conformable unto his death."* This is what the writer meant when he said: *"Let us go forth therefore unto him without the camp, bearing his reproach"* (Hebrews 13:13). If we are to know Christ personally, we must stay close to Him and identify with Him. And how can we know Him if we never draw near to Him?

Jesus said:

I am the good shepherd, and know my sheep, and am known of mine.
John 10:14

My sheep hear my voice, and I know them, and they follow me.
John 10:27

There is no other way to know God. Draw near to Him today.

Other Important Elements in Our Quest to Know Christ

Another element that is important to our quest to know Christ more fully was explored by the apostle John in his letters to the young churches of the first century:

Whosoever abideth in him sinneth not: whosoever sinneth hath not seen him, neither known him.
1 John 3:6

The person who would know God in His fullness must stop practicing sin, for saying that we love Him and continuing to hurt Him by our willfulness and disobedience is somehow contradictory. Sin and intimacy with God do not go together, for they are like oil and water. No one who lives in Christ's fullness keeps on sinning, and no one who continues to sin has either seen Him or known Him.

8

It is interesting to note that when teaching on this subject, John used such precise and strict language. This is serious business. You cannot know God if you continue to sin. Period!

John revealed another element that is essential to our knowing God:

Beloved, let us love one another: for love is of God; and every one that loveth is born of God, and knoweth God. He that loveth not knoweth not God; for God is love.

1 John 4:7-8

This, of course, speaks of agape love, which is devotion or dedication to one another. If I love someone, it means that I am devoted to him and to his well-being. This kind of love comes only from God.

Agape is such an important subject that I have dedicated an entire chapter to it in this book, but I must say a little about it here because of John's insistence that we cannot know God without it. As we shall see, it seems that even the Pharisees had a measure of agape love. Everybody has some of it because we are born with it. The problem is not that we have no agape love, but that we misdirect our love in ways God did not intend. So what was John saying with such boldness?

He was saying that everyone who loves in the way God intended has been born of Him and knows Him, and whoever does not love as God intended does not know God because He *is* love. If I am not devoted to you and your well-being, I do not know God, and I can never know God. Isn't that a powerful truth? It is one that all too often is skimmed over without receiving the attention it deserves.

My place here on earth (and yours as well) is to love and serve Christ, and if we love and serve Him, we must also love and serve one another. The Scriptures are clear on this point. In His message on the judging of the nations, Jesus said:

Becoming the Expression of the Father

For I was an hungred, and ye gave me no meat: I was thirsty, and ye gave me no drink: I was a stranger, and ye took me not in: naked, and ye clothed me not: sick, and in prison, and ye visited me not. Then shall they also answer him, saying, Lord, when saw we thee an hungred, or athirst, or a stranger, or naked, or sick, or in prison, and did not minister unto thee? Then shall he answer them, saying, Verily I say unto you, Inasmuch as ye did it not to one of the least of these, ye did it not to me. And these shall go away into everlasting punishment: but the righteous into life eternal.

Matthew 25:42-46

Jesus came as a loving servant, and if we cannot become loving servants and live as loving servants, no place will be found for us among His chosen ones. We certainly will never attain to the high calling God has in mind for us. If even Jesus did not come to be ministered to, but to minister (see Matthew 20:28), what can we expect as a requirement for life?

Don't worry. Jesus was ministered to, and you will be too. Otherwise you would have nothing to offer to others. But being ministered *to* is never your purpose. You must live to serve if you are to know Christ fully.

*You must live to serve if you are
to know Christ fully.*

One of the reasons that we often fail to serve others as we should is that we are preoccupied building our own place in the kingdom. This is an error. We must be loving servants, whatever that requires of us at the moment.

Our Expectations for the Future

Although I have been blessed to serve the Lord in several capacities through the years, I am not expecting to have a throne waiting for me in heaven. I would not know what to do with it. I would rather wash someone's feet there, and I expect to remain a servant throughout eternity.

My greatest excitement about the future is the fact that I will see the Lord face to face, and also that I will be *"like Him"*:

> *Beloved, now are we the sons of God, and it doth not yet appear what we shall be: but we know that, when he shall appear, we shall be like him; for we shall see him as he is. And every man that hath this hope in him purifieth himself, even as he is pure.*
>
> 1 John 3:2-3

It should be apparent to all of us that what we shall be has not yet been manifested. At this point, how do we even know what we may become in God as we know Him better? The fullness of who we are in Him may become known down here in part, but the real unveiling will come only on the other side.

There will surely be many surprises on that day. Some of those whom we have thought will be very important in the kingdom will undoubtedly have a lower place than we imagined, and many whom we have not recognized as great may well have a much higher place than we would have assigned to them. Thank God that He is the faithful Judge of all things. Only He can know the true level of our commitment to Him.

One thing we do know. When He is fully revealed, we will not only *see* Him as He is, but we also will *be* like Him. And that is a glorious thought!

But there is a qualifying factor: *"every man that hath this hope in him purifieth himself, even as he is pure."* Does every man purify himself to the same degree? Surely not.

Becoming the Expression of the Father

I see another qualifying factor in the original text of 1 John 3:2 that helps me to better understand the passage. Darby's Translation, which I feel does a better job of conveying the meaning of the original Greek, says it this way:

> *Beloved, now are we children of God, and what we shall be has not yet been manifested; we know that if it is manifested we shall be like him, for we shall see him as he is.*
>
> 1 John 3:2 DT

There is an *"if"* here: *"if it is manifested."* My feeling is that how much we come to know Christ and how much we allow Him to be manifested to us and through us down here will ultimately determine how much like Him we will be up there. Jude had a prayer for each believer that shows God's will in the matter:

> *Now unto him that is able to keep you from falling, and to present you faultless before the presence of his glory with exceeding joy, to the only wise God our Saviour, be glory and majesty, dominion and power, both now and ever. Amen.*
>
> Jude 24-25

The goal is *"to present you faultless before the presence of his glory."* How wonderful! No wonder Paul felt that things were not to be greatly valued here and that anything was dispensable in order to gain Christ. No wonder he considered that his sufferings in this life were not even worthy to be mentioned in the light of his goal to know Christ (see Romans 8:18).

But, as I will show in the next chapter, I am convinced that not every believer knows Christ to the same degree. In fact, I am sure of it. I am also sure that this fact will be reflected in the ultimate destiny of every single one of us. To what extent will the glory of God reside in you throughout eternity? To what extent will you be transformed into the image of God's dear Son? In my humble way of thinking, it will be to the same extent to which you have come to know His person in the here and now.

✦ ≓✦≓ ✦

Your spiritual investments will pay off for all eternity.

✦ ≓✦≓ ✦

Whatever price you have to pay to accomplish that transformation will be meaningless. Nothing that you could possibly possess here could be worth more than knowing Christ. All the things you have accumulated in life will soon have very little value, but your spiritual investments will pay off for all eternity. You have the promise:

> *And the world passeth away, and the lust thereof: but he that doeth the will of God abideth for ever.*
>
> 1 John 2:17

Those who choose to pay the price to know Christ more fully will themselves be chosen to show forth His power and love here on earth. They will become the expression of the Father.

Becoming the Expression of the Father

Chapter Two

CHOOSING BETWEEN THE BROAD AND THE NARROW WAYS

Enter ye in at the strait gate: for wide is the gate, and broad is the way, that leadeth to destruction, and many there be which go in thereat: because strait is the gate, and narrow is the way, which leadeth unto life, and few there be that find it.

Matthew 7:13-14

Usually we have related this teaching of Jesus only to the difference between the saved and the lost. But I am convinced that there is more here than meets the eye.

Far too many Christians, I fear, have chosen to walk on the broad way. This may explain why their Christian experience is not as rich as they imagined it might be. Those who walk the broad way (even if they do obtain salvation) lose much of what the Lord has in store for them. By choosing the easy pathway through life, they miss the very best of what life has to offer.

Becoming the Expression of the Father

It is possible to be a Christian and still spend your time and resources exactly as you want to. It is possible to be a Christian and still go where you want to go and do what you want to do. It is possible to be a Christian and to ask God to bless your choices in life and still go about doing your own thing. But if you choose this easy and popular path, you will surely not know the Lord Jesus in His fullness. His way is one of denial of our wills and of acceptance of His better will for us.

Although it is possible to go to church when you want to and give what you want to and still make heaven your home, those who choose this path cannot expect to have God's very best. They will surely have a lot of tears that will need to be wiped away once they get to heaven.

Those Who Are to Be Cast Into "Outer Darkness"

Like the broad versus the narrow way, there is another biblical term that we normally use in reference to the lost that I believe has a much different application. It is the term *"outer darkness."* This term is found only in the book of Matthew and even there only three times. In the first instance, it is used in reference to *"the children of the kingdom"*:

> But the children of the kingdom shall be cast out into outer darkness: there shall be weeping and gnashing of teeth.
>
> Matthew 8:12

If they are *"children of the kingdom,"* then this surely does not refer to the unrighteous or the wicked. Still, although the people in question are obviously related to God's kingdom in some way, they will be *"cast out into outer darkness."* This is a serious matter that deserves more of our consideration.

In the second use of the term *"outer darkness"* in the Bible, a man was invited to a wedding, but he arrived without the customary wedding garment:

16

And when the king came in to see the guests, he saw there a man which had not on a wedding garment: and he saith unto him, Friend, how camest thou in hither not having a wedding garment? And he was speechless. Then said the king to the servants, Bind him hand and foot, and take him away, and cast him into outer darkness; there shall be weeping and gnashing of teeth. For many are called, but few are chosen.

Matthew 22:11-14

The fact that the man was an invited guest and that he was called *"friend"* seems to me to indicate that he was not an unbeliever. Still, he was to be cast *"into outer darkness"*—because he was not prepared. Again, this is serious business. We must make ourselves ready. John declared to the church:

Let us be glad and rejoice, and give honour to him: for the marriage of the Lamb is come, and his wife hath made herself ready.

Revelation 19:7

When John said, *"his wife hath made herself ready,"* he was not referring to our salvation. We do not just wake up one day and decide to get out of the gutter and clean ourselves up so that we can be acceptable to God. Our salvation is precipitated by God Himself. It is He who comes to us in the gutter, stretches out His hand, and offers to lift us up. So, in the sense of salvation, there is nothing we can do to make ourselves ready. Only He can do that. When John spoke of the bride having made herself ready, therefore, he was not speaking of her salvation, but of her adorning:

And to her was granted that she should be arrayed in fine linen, clean and white: for the fine linen is the righteousness of saints.

Revelation 19:8

The bride of Christ is to be like a city set on a hill. She is to be a light to many. She is to be an example to others around her. Nations will walk in her light. And all this will be true only because she has made herself ready. She has qualified. She has developed through the grace and mercy of God, and she has become what He purposed her to be from the beginning.

The garment that the bride wears is not, as many have suggested, the garment of salvation. It is a wedding garment, and it is made up of the righteous acts of the saints. The bride is working the works of God. Righteous acts, although they can never save us, can qualify us for a higher place in God's eternity. And they can bring us into His inner circle.

Righteous acts can qualify us for a higher place in God's eternity.

It is time to mature so that we will be ready for our future assignments. The Song of Solomon speaks of a young woman who was unprepared to be betrothed:

We have a little sister, and she hath no breasts: what shall we do for our sister in the day when she shall be spoken for?

Song of Solomon 8:8

How embarrassing! And the worst was yet to come. Some man would eventually say to her father, "I think it's time for your daughter to consider marriage, and I'm offering my son as a suitable groom." But the father would not know what to answer, for his daughter, alas, would be too immature for marriage.

The Song of Solomon continued:

If she be a wall, we will build upon her a palace of silver: and if she be a door, we will inclose her with boards of cedar.

Song of Solomon 8:9

In other words, if she were something else, a wall or a door, her brothers could think of something to do with her. But she was not a wall or a door; she was a young woman, and a young woman in those days and in those cultural settings should think of marriage and children. But to marry this young woman off to some unsuspecting man was out of the question. She was too immature to serve as either wife or mother.

The bride our Lord is seeking will be fully developed in godly character and inner beauty, purity, and holiness. She will be established in God and conformed to the image of Christ. Only then will she find favor in His sight. He will say to her:

Rise up, my love, my fair one, and come away.

Arise, my love, my fair one, and come away.

Song of Solomon 2:10, 13

To an unprepared woman, such things could never be said. So, the choice is ours. Now is the time to prepare.

In the third use of the term *"outer darkness,"* a man who is to be cast *"into outer darkness"* is called a *"servant,"* although an *"unprofitable"* one:

And cast ye the unprofitable servant into outer darkness: there shall be weeping and gnashing of teeth.

Matthew 25:30

The story is that a man entrusted his talents to several servants, and then he went away on a journey. This particular servant took the talent entrusted to him, put it into a box, and buried it in the ground for safekeeping. He did nothing with it, showing that he was unworthy of it.

God requires that we appreciate His gifts and that we show our appreciation by utilizing them for good. This is not just for the sake of accomplishment. If God just wanted work done, He could employ His legions of angels to do it. Getting the work done is not the point.

19

Becoming the Expression of the Father

The point is that He has entrusted certain responsibilities into our care and keeping, and what we do with them will show Him our true character and how much He can trust us with in days to come.

To the other servants, those who used well the talents entrusted to them, the Lord said, *"Well done, thou good and faithful servant: thou hast been faithful over a few things, I will make thee ruler over many things: enter thou into the joy of thy lord"* (Matthew 25:21, 23). These servants would now have authority to function in a greater capacity, and it was because they had proven themselves qualified to serve in that way.

The conclusion we must reach from examining these three passages is that the term *"outer darkness"* was never used by Jesus in reference to the wicked. So what did Jesus mean by these words? In them I sense great loss—not necessarily hell, as most people interpret them. I would describe the act of being cast into outer darkness as being cast out of the light, out of the center of activity.

In the cultural atmosphere in which the Bible was written, there was limited light available during nighttime, and this almost always was associated with dwellings. Beyond the limited light used in individual dwellings, all was darkness in the land. This may well be the *"outer darkness"* of which Jesus spoke.

So what does it mean to us? If we are to know the Lord in His fullness, we cannot remain far from His light. And how close we stay to His light will determine our level of maturity and trustworthiness.

A Dream About Heaven

I once had a dream in which I saw myself with a group of people being conducted from place to place by an angel. We seemed to be in heaven. We came to one room that looked very much like a church, for it had pews similar to those we use in our churches today. People dressed in many different ways were sitting scattered throughout those pews. There was no unified activity and no leader, and everyone seemed to be doing whatever he or she wanted to do at the moment. Some were facing the front, but others were talking among themselves.

Aside from there being no unity in that place, I could sense that there was not much happening there in the spirit realm either. I seemed to have special insight into the people who were in the church-like room and could sense what they were like, what was inside of them, and I did not like what I was seeing. These people seemed shallow. I was transfixed by this fact and very surprised, to say the least.

The thought of having to stay in that room terrified me so much that I was nearly frozen with dread. I thought, *Surely I don't have to stay here!* But I couldn't be sure.

The angel had left three or four of us there and had turned to go on with the others. When I saw several of them going out through the door, I rushed to follow. My heart pounded in my chest as I moved toward the door. For some reason, I was afraid that the door would be locked to me. I was relieved to find that it was still open, and I rushed through it.

I called to the angel, "May I come with you?"

"If you want to," the angel answered.

I wanted to, and I hurried to catch up with the rest of the group.

We came to another room that looked like a Greek theater. It had a stage in front, and the seating area contained backless, marble benches. Everything was decorated in shades of white. This time, the people (who also were all dressed in white) were all facing the front, and there was a leader present who was addressing them. I gravitated down toward the front to see a robe that had been rolled up and laid out in a "u" shape.

I felt happier in this place, and it seemed that I could stay there. I sensed the Spirit there, there was unity among the people, and they seemed to have real direction (no one seemed to be just doing what he or she wanted to do at the moment). Everybody was in tune with the leader and in tune with the Spirit and the worship, and there was a definite direction toward the Lord. I liked that and felt that I could be happy there.

Becoming the Expression of the Father

As it turned out, I did not stay in that place either. The angel came and got me out of my seat and said that we were going to yet another level.

I never got to that other level. Instead I found myself back on earth on a highway in the middle of some heavy traffic. I sensed that I was being examined to see if I would qualify for a higher level. The examination was to see how I would react to earth's situations and if those situations had worked enough quality into my life. Did I have enough patience? How did I respond to life's ups and downs, and what did they bring about in me? If I passed this test, I understood, I would then be able to go on to another level.

This dream taught me that there are degrees, levels, or divisions (call them whatever you want) in the kingdom of God. This should not surprise us. Our earthly governments are complex in structure, and the kingdom of heaven is a much more complex government than any on earth.

Normally we would not need to know about these things, but since we are part of the complexity of God's kingdom and since we will each function in a specific role there, the Lord is training us for what we will do in eternity. Get used to it; we all are in training.

Some, I am afraid, will choose to walk such a broad path down here that they will not make the grade for a coveted place up there. They will not qualify for what God has prepared for them, and they will have to take a lesser position than is their rightful inheritance. Again, this may cause them some tears, but God will wipe them all away—as He has promised. I am sure that eventually we will all settle down and be quite content in heaven, but the loss some suffer because of their failure to prepare adequately will be great.

⊷⊶⊷

We are in training now for eternity.

⊷⊶⊷

Choose to pay the necessary price now because you are here in this life for only a short time. Then begins eternity. Here God is testing us, trying us, so that we can qualify for what He has for us in the days to come. But crowns are not souvenirs that are easily acquired; they must be earned.

The fact that there are varying positions, levels, or degrees in God's kingdom does not show a bias on His part. His desire is to move each of us upward into higher realms, and we can either hinder or facilitate those desires. In the end, it will not depend on others and how well they liked us. It will all depend on our individual determination to know God better and to fully perform His will.

Degrees Already at Work

Among Christians living today, we can already see some of the varying degrees of dedication at work. In any given group of believers we can see many different spiritual levels. For instance, if you were to examine ten believers who came to the Lord at about the same time (meaning that they all have about the same number of years of experience in Him) you might be surprised to find a great degree of difference in the level of maturity among them. All of them may be in the kingdom, but some are definitely closer to God than others.

Why and how does that happen? It is because of the choices people make in life. Some are satisfied with little, while others choose to go the extra mile. Some avoid anything painful or potentially threatening, while others choose to go through the fire of trials and tests. Some choose to maintain their lives as much like they were before their conversion to Christ as possible, while others are ready to cast everything aside to discover better ways in Him. Some give themselves completely, while others hold back. As a result, at the end of ten years, the corresponding levels of maturity are all over the map.

Becoming the Expression of the Father

Why do some get closer to God than others? It is apparent that they have paid the price to accomplish it. Why was Moses allowed to draw near to God, while others had to stand at a distance? Surely God is no respecter of persons? He isn't. The choice is ours, not His. Don't wait until it is too late to understand this principle. Start doing whatever is necessary today to know God more fully. Your future is at stake.

When all is said and done, we will have no one but ourselves to blame for whatever lack of progress is found in us. It would be very easy to blame our slow progress on some enemy or other. But if the truth were to be told, I am my own worst enemy. We are always quick to blame the devil, but I have problems that are far greater than anything he can muster up. The biggest problem I face every day is dealing with myself—even when the devil seems to be nowhere in sight. If there is someone who gets in the way, it is me—not the devil.

Many have not pressed into God's best because they are satisfied with the good things He has already given them. In this way, the good actually prevents them from attaining the better and the best. How sad! How about you? Will you choose to walk the broad way, the popular path, or will you insist on traveling the narrow path to greatness? Those who choose to narrow their focus in this life will be chosen to become the expression of the Father.

Chapter Three

STANDING BEFORE THE LORD

And Elijah the Tishbite, who was of the inhabitants of Gilead, said unto Ahab, As the LORD God of Israel liveth, before whom I stand...

1 Kings 17:1

It is interesting that when Elijah appeared for the first time in the Scriptures, he had been standing before the Lord. That speaks highly of the prophet because standing before the Lord is a very good place to be indeed.

When we stand before the Lord, we don't get tired, for we receive of His strength and energy. And we receive much more. Elijah, for instance, was not afraid to speak boldly to the wicked King Ahab because he was receiving God's boldness as he stood before Him.

That men would stand before Him was not only God's will for Elijah and the ancient prophets, but His will for you and me today as well. The closer we can get to Him, the better. When we are in that place of standing, we suddenly begin to see things from God's perspective. And what could be more important? This is more true now than it ever has been.

But when you stand before the Lord, do so not out of a desire to receive something specific (for instance, direction for some particular decision), but out of a desire to know Him better. Many times we are driven by a desire to have something from God or to know His will for a particular situation. But He does not always want us to know it fully (at least, not at the moment). What He wants is for us to know Him better.

The Place of Knowing God's Will

God's will is your business only when He chooses to make it your business. If He does not do that, then it is wrong for you to insist on prying into His affairs. Stop trying to prematurely know things and let God reveal them to you in His time. Just concentrate on getting to know Him, and He will show you all that you need to know at the moment.

My earthly father was never bashful about letting me and the rest of our family know what his will was (what he wanted and expected from us), and neither is my heavenly Father. Knowing God's will is not a problem—if He wants you to know it.

My earthly father did not consider it to be my responsibility to ask about what he wanted or expected, and he would let me know that fact in no uncertain terms. If he wanted me to know something, he would tell me. If he did not tell me, then it was none of my business.

When he did tell me what he wanted, I knew that I had better listen carefully and obey him fully, or I would experience his wrath. It did not take me long to learn that his will was important, and this stood me in good stead when it came time to relate to my heavenly Father.

Many Christians are lax concerning the will of God. They move ahead of Him, and they always want Him to reveal to them something or other in which He has no interest at all. Your interests are not necessarily His interests, so you need to forget yours and learn His.

When I came to know the Lord, I said to Him, "I will do Your will, with one condition: that You always let me know what it is." That approach worked. He has let me know consistently what He wanted, and I have tried to follow Him faithfully.

I was tested on my commitment when I was still very young and in Bible school. I arrived home one evening to find that my younger brother Wilfred had been smitten with polio. It was by now about six p.m., and he had been attacked around two that afternoon. By the time I got home, he was lying on the couch unable to walk. The pain in his feet was so intense that he could not stand the sheet to touch them.

The doctor had been there and said that it looked to him like a severe case of polio. He would have a room prepared in the local hospital, and my brother would be admitted the next morning.

Here was my brother, someone I loved, my own flesh and blood, suffering. I sat down with my heart screaming. What would happen to him? He could die. At the very best, he would probably become a semi-invalid. I began to talk to God about the situation.

"God, what do You want?" I asked.

He knew what I wanted, for He could hear the screaming of my heart, but I was willing for His will to be done in the matter instead of mine.

"God, if You want to take him, I'll go along with that. If You want him to be crippled all his life, I'll go along with that, too. But if You want to heal him, that would be wonderful!"

I was determined to accept His will—whatever it happened to be—with my whole heart. His decision might break my heart, but I would live and be blessed.

Then the presence of God came upon me like fire moving through my feet, and in that burning fire was the knowledge of the will of God to raise my brother up.

I got up from where I was sitting, walked over to the couch, and put my hand on him. Instantly, he was up and walking like nothing had happened.

This was the confirmation that I had indeed heard from God and known His will in the matter. It came because I had been walking with the Lord even as I went about the part-time job I had started at a grocery store.

Stop trying to pry loose from the fingers of God things that do not pertain to you and that He does not want to release to you just yet. That is dangerous. He is not being formed to become your expression in the earth; it is just the opposite. So stop trying to insist that God agree with what you want to do. Listen to what He has to say as you stand before Him and get to know His heart. Then you will know the will of God—or as much of it as He wants you to know at any given moment.

The Place of Revelation and Provision

Standing in God's presence is the place of revelation. To know Him is to know His truth and to know the ways in which He leads and guides. Knowing Him is to know His voice, and knowing His voice is to come to know His will. To know Him is to know all that you need to know when you need to know it.

> *Standing in God's presence is the place of revelation.*

Elijah is a good example of this. As he was standing before the Lord on a certain day, he learned something—that there would soon be a drought in the land. Where did such an idea come from? Not out of his own head surely. It came to him from the heart of God.

Next, after knowing what was about to take place, Elijah could receive direction about what he should do about it. This was where the prophet learned. It was the way Elijah operated, and it is the way every true prophet operates. And just as Elijah's direction came from his position before the Lord, that is where ours should come from today.

That particular day, as he stood humbly before the Lord, *"the word of the LORD came unto him"* (1 Kings 17:2). The word was this:

Get thee hence, and turn thee eastward, and hide thyself by the brook Cherith, that is before Jordan. And it shall be, that thou shalt drink of the brook; and I have commanded the ravens to feed thee there.

1 Kings 17:3-4

This is typical of the way God speaks. He is very specific and detailed, and He leaves nothing to chance. And with His instruction always comes a means of provision for His servant.

Notice that God had commanded the ravens to feed Elijah *"there,"* nowhere else. I like that. God is very specific, and when we obey Him, He supplies our needs. But if we fail to be *"there,"* in the specific place God has revealed to us as we draw near to Him and feel His heartbeat, we may not have what we need on a daily basis. If we are not *"there,"* we will never even see the ravens, let alone receive from them.

This is important, so don't be guilty of minimizing it. In order to have your daily needs supplied, you must be at your *"there,"* and your *"there"* is not wherever you decide it is. Your *"there"* must come out from the heart of God, not from within yourself. So you will only know your *"there"* if you are standing close enough to Him to hear it when He chooses to reveal it to you.

The next words recorded are also important:

Becoming the Expression of the Father

So he went and did according unto the word of the LORD: for he went and dwelt by the brook Cherith, that is before Jordan.

1 Kings 17:5

First, Elijah got close to God and listened, and then he "went and did" what God had told him to do. Therefore, we should not be surprised that his miracle came. Ravens sustained him during the entire period of drought.

It has often been said that Elijah stayed by the brook until the water dried up and the ravens stopped coming to feed him, but the truth is that he stayed there until the word of the Lord came to him to do something different. That is the key. As we will see in much greater detail later on in the book, we are never to be guided by negative circumstances but by the heart of God. That guarantees success every time.

God does not guarantee your keep when you are doing what you want to do where you want to do it. His miracle supply operates in your *"there"*—wherever that happens to be at the moment. That which God ordains is always blessed, but that which you decide upon may not be.

At one point Paul and his companions had determined to go into Asia, but the Spirit did not allow it. Then they decided to go to Bithynia, *"but the Spirit suffered them not"*:

Now when they had gone throughout Phrygia and the region of Galatia, and were forbidden of the Holy Ghost to preach the word in Asia, after they were come to Mysia, they assayed to go into Bithynia: but the Spirit suffered them not.

Acts 16:6-7

As they prayed about what to do, a vision came to Paul of a man from Macedonia, and he suddenly knew where they should go and what they should do. In doing it, they would be provided for and protected, so they went without fear.

Isaiah also spoke of this kind of merciful guidance:

And thine ears shall hear a word behind thee, saying, This is the way, walk ye in it.

Isaiah 30:21

This passage speaks of those who have returned to the paths of the Lord and are currently walking on the right road. As they walk, they hear the Lord's voice guiding their steps. When this is our case, we, like Elijah, can have no fear.

The Place of No Fear

Because Elijah stood before the Lord and received revelation and direction for his life, all the things he normally would have been afraid of and worried about did not bother him at all. When we know that God is in the details, we have nothing to fear. For instance, when Elijah learned that Ahab was hunting him to take his life, he decided to do a very bold thing. He went to Ahab and confronted him personally:

And Elijah said, As the LORD of hosts liveth, before whom I stand, I will surely shew myself unto him [Ahab] *to day.*

1 Kings 18:15

What Elijah was about to do was fairly death-defying, but he was not worried. When you live close to God, you can stare death in the face and not blink. I experienced it myself many times during the years we were living and working among the primitive tribes of Peru.

One day, for instance, three canoe loads of native Indian men rushed into our compound, intent on killing. This was obvious in that they had brought no women or children with them, and they were adorned in war paint and dress. I prayed a quick prayer about what I should do and decided to go out and meet them like I was greeting old friends.

Becoming the Expression of the Father

I was not sure if I might be their intended victim. As it turned out, I wasn't. It was someone else they wanted, someone who happened not to be around at the moment. But the fact that I had no fear as I went out to meet them that day was a wonderful feeling. Only knowing God and knowing where we stand in Him can give us that fearlessness in the face of danger.

The first time I visited that tribe, it was in the midst of a terrible plague. Most of the people were severely ill and some had recently died. A wrapped body hung elevated from the ground, and a fire under it smoked it in preparation for burial. Others would soon die.

There was little food in the camp because the men had been too sick to go out hunting recently. Someone had prepared a huge pot of yucca (by now stale), and anyone who was well enough to eat simply helped themselves to it. For the most part, no one seemed to be eating.

A young boy whose belly was severely distended from worm infestation got out of his hammock and defecated on the dirt floor of the hut where I was staying. Two mangy dogs quickly appeared and began eating the human feces. A woman chased them out of the room, but on their way out, they passed the big pot of yucca sitting in the dirt, and they plunged their faces into it and ate ravenously.

The woman saw what was happening and chased the dogs away from the pot. Seeing the pot apparently reminded her that I, their recently arrived guest, might be hungry. She went to the pot (from which the dogs had just eaten after having eaten the human feces) and dipped out a bowl of the cooked yucca and brought it to me.

I had seen it all and was sure that the dogs had deposited some of what they had been eating previously in the food, and now I had a decision to make. If I rejected what was being offered to me, I knew that I could not reach these people for Christ. And that was what I had been called to do. It did not make good sense hygienically to eat

32

the yucca, but to not eat it would have been such an offense to the people that I felt I could not even consider it.

Instead, I took the red clay bowl that was offered to me and I held it up to God. "Lord," I prayed, "You see this, and You know what's in it. I'm going to eat it—if You don't stop me."

He did not stop me, and I ate the yucca and suffered no ill from it. But I had to know where I stood with God that day. If I hadn't, I would never have had the courage to do such a thing.

Nothing is more important than being in the center of the will of God and knowing where you stand with Him. It not only brings you clear direction for your life but also an assurance that everything will be okay.

While living in Iquitos, Peru, we used a houseboat to make trips up and down the Amazon and its tributaries. We had to be cautious because it was not uncommon for children to be taken by the large boa constrictors that frequented those waterways. These reptiles could reach fifteen feet or more in length. Friends of ours had lost a six-year-old boy that way. By the time the father was able to reach the scene, the boy had been crushed and was already half swallowed by the snake. Imagine how terrible it must have been for that father to see his son in such a situation!

One day our children were playing in a shallow part of the river. They were unaware of any danger, but a native woman who had come to draw water saw a large boa lurking in the water near them and screamed for them to get out immediately. They were able to scramble out in time, but the boa continued to lurk around and under the houseboat.

We told the children not to play in the river for a while, but a few days later, our four-year-old daughter Brenda was playing in a dugout canoe tied up at the water's edge. The canoe was about eighteen feet long, and she was at the back part of it where there was a small platform that extended near the surface of the water. Somehow she lost her balance and fell into the water.

Becoming the Expression of the Father

The disturbance attracted the boa, and it came swimming quickly toward Brenda. Fortunately, a white domesticated duck happened along at that very moment and swam between Brenda and the rapidly approaching snake. As the duck rounded the back corner of the canoe it was snatched by the boa and quickly disappeared under water. While the snake wrestled the duck, Brenda was able to scramble out of the water.

I had had enough of that boa constrictor. We quickly got some long fishing spears and began jabbing into the three- or-four-foot deep water trying to locate him. When we had successfully sunk a couple of those spears into his hide, he released the duck and coiled around the grass on the bottom of the river. We tried to dislodge him but lost one spear in the process.

This left only one spear holding the heavy reptile, but with that spear, we were finally able to force him to break water. He was not finished by any measure, and this threat forced him to exert more strength, and he began pulling himself loose from the one spear that had been holding him. It was apparent that he would soon escape if something was not done. Then he would have further opportunity to threaten our children.

I felt that I could not permit that, and I sensed that God did not want us to be defeated in this situation. We simply could not permit the snake to escape. Without thinking, I jumped into the water and, with my bare hands, grabbed the snake by its tail and began to wrestle its weight onto land.

It never occurred to me in that moment that I was now putting myself in danger. I had a great sense of power and sufficiency in God, and interestingly enough, I felt no fear at all.

I was on my own, though, for the natives would not help me. To them, the boa constrictor was the third most powerful spirit in the jungle. They would stand and cheer me on, but they would never touch the creature.

For some reason, the sixteen-foot snake (as we later measured it to be) was helpless in my hands that day. He did not even attempt to turn on me. He did defecate on me at one point, but other than that, it was apparent that I would be the victor. With what seemed to be little effort, I flung the huge beast out of the water and onto the dry ground—where he was easily killed.

As I thought on my victory that day, I remembered young David. He knew where he stood when he faced the bear and the lion, and he knew where he stood when he went out against Goliath. We must never expect that when we have been standing before the Lord, we will not encounter problems in life. But standing before the Lord prepares us for life's problems, and we can then face them as if they were nothing.

Facing enemies after you have stood before the Lord is a pleasure, not a terror. You will do it in God, and your victory will come from Him. There is no enemy that He cannot help you face—when you take time to know Him more intimately.

Finding God Where He Is Least Expected

As Elijah stood before the Lord, he was not sure exactly how God would speak to him:

And he said, Go forth, and stand upon the mount before the LORD. And, behold, the LORD passed by, and a great and strong wind rent the mountains, and brake in pieces the rocks before the LORD; but the LORD was not in the wind: and after the wind an earthquake; but the LORD was not in the earthquake: and after the earthquake a fire; but the LORD was not in the fire: and after the fire a still small voice.

1 Kings 19:11-12

Like Elijah, we look for the Lord in many places, expecting Him to be there, and we are disappointed when He is not. In this case, He was not in the wind, He was not in the earthquake, and He was

35

not in the fire. But when God did not speak through the wind, the earthquake, or the fire, Elijah kept listening intently and did not miss hearing God in the *"still small voice."*

Do not limit God. He is so awesome that He has created a world within every tiny human cell. Our most powerful microscopes have not yet been able to delve to the depths of such a cell, and, we are told, it would require a thousand binders with six hundred pages of text each to fully describe the functions carried out in just one of these cells. That is how great our God is.

In that one human cell, we are told, there is a thread that could reach to the sun and back to Earth again—and not just once or even twice—but four hundred times. Imagine it! Our God can be seen in the vastness of the universe, but also in the complexity of the simplest cell.

Don't limit God, and don't just expect to hear His voice in one place and in one way. Go on to know all the various levels in Him. You won't run out, for they are endless.

✦ ❈✦❈ ✦

You will never run out of levels of knowing God.

✦ ❈✦❈ ✦

Limited human creatures that we are, we often limit God and expect to hear from Him in some certain way. Once, for instance, a brother took it upon himself to raise money to send me to Israel, but I really did not have a desire to go at the time. I prayed that he would not be successful, and he wasn't.

He had given me some money as he had raised it, and I was about to return it all to him when another friend began telling me that I really should take a ministry trip to Europe. He had contacts there. In fact, he planned to go himself, and he said we could meet in England.

"What do I want to go to Europe for?" I asked, and despite the fact that he had other arguments for such a trip, I said, "No, I'm not going."

But the idea began to "bug" me, and my unease grew until I felt like I simply had to go. I had no choice in the matter.

Still, I was uncomfortable with the way the whole thing had come about. I was accustomed to receiving a clear leading from the Lord about what I should do and then moving on that word. This was different. So, before I left for Europe, I wanted the Lord to speak to me more clearly.

I prayed, and I explained to the Lord what I was feeling. There was pressure from somewhere for me to go, and I felt that I had no choice, but I was just stubborn enough to want to have some more precise direction. When none came, I finally said to the Lord, "God, I'm going to go, but if I'm making a mistake, please stop me before I get too far. I trust Your faithfulness to me." No answer came.

The time to leave arrived, and I had received no word from heaven. As I flew to Germany on the first leg of the trip, I rather expected to receive something concrete in the air six miles above the earth, but it did not come.

Was God hearing me? I wondered.

God manifested Himself to the people I ministered to in Germany, but the messenger felt alone and neglected. God did not seem to be speaking to me for some reason, and I could not understand why.

As I moved through my appointed itinerary, I looked for God to show me something, but He did not. By the time my plane lifted off from Northern Ireland to return me to the United States at the end of the tour, I had reached the conclusion that I had made a terrible mistake by making the trip in the first place, and I was saddened by that thought.

Then, as the wheels of the plane touched down in Pittsburgh, a great presence of the Lord came over me, and the Spirit of the Lord said the strangest thing to me: "Thank you." In that moment, I knew that I had passed the test. I had been willing to be sent out, even when I felt that somehow God had stayed home and sent me alone.

Becoming the Expression of the Father

It was Him doing the work. He poured into the people. He gave out to them. I was just His obedient vessel, even when I was no longer feeling His hugs. Let God be God. Stand beside Him, and allow Him to express Himself as He will.

To Stand Also Means to Continue

The same word translated in these passages as "standing" is translated a little differently in Psalm 119:

They continue this day according to thine ordinances: for all are thy servants.

Psalm 119:91

To stand then is to continue. Understanding this can help the thinking of those of us who feel that standing before the Lord is a place of inactivity and are bothered by that fact. After all, inactivity does not seem to be compatible with being the Lord's servants. But would we say that a great tree is unproductive just because it stands and continues to stand? Certainly not. In fact, a tree produces so much fruit in its lifetime and reproduces itself so many times over that it is difficult for the mind to take it all in.

The secret is that a tree does a lot while it just seems to be standing there. For one thing, it lifts hundreds of gallons of water a day to its extremities. And that is just part of the internal workings of a tree. It does a lot more than that. Meantime, it just keeps standing there. This is why the Lord has said:

Ye shall not need to fight in this battle: set yourselves, stand ye still, and see the salvation of the LORD with you, O Judah and Jerusalem: fear not, nor be dismayed; to-morrow go out against them: for the LORD will be with you.

2 Chronicles 20:17

This certainly did not indicate the need for inactivity on the part of God's people, but rather that they did not need to fight the battle in their own strength.

38

But times of inactivity are not all bad. Some of us are so busy doing things for God that we have no time to listen to Him. Samuel asked Saul to *"stand...still a while"* so that he could show him what God wanted to say:

> *And as they were going down to the end of the city, Samuel said to Saul, Bid the servant pass on before us, (and he passed on,) but stand thou still a while, that I may shew thee the word of God.*
>
> 1 Samuel 9:27

Why did Saul's servant *"pass on"* when the word of the Lord was about to be revealed? Evidently he was too busy serving to de delayed. This should not surprise us. Jesus sometimes had to do something special to get His disciples to come aside and hear His word. He would send them out to deal with the sick and cast out devils and get all the service out of their systems so that they could then sit still for a while, and He could speak to them privately and personally.

One day He was speaking to them about the need to refine their personal relationships with each other, and right in the middle of His teaching, Peter interrupted Him and said, *"Increase our faith"* (Luke 17:5). Jesus answered, *"If ye had faith..."* (verse 6). If Peter had had any faith, he would have realized that what Jesus was teaching them was important and not to be interrupted.

For most of us, standing still is just too difficult. We would rather be doing something. After all, what will we tell our friends we have accomplished? But Jesus preferred that His disciples be His friends more than just His servants:

> *Henceforth I call you not servants; for the servant knoweth not what his lord doeth: but I have called you friends; for all things that I have heard of my Father I have made known unto you.*
>
> John 15:15

Becoming the Expression of the Father

Servants are often too busy to sit by the Master's side. They often have no time to hear His word. Stand still, and He will speak to you.

People pray in different ways, but most of the time that I spend before the Lord is done in absolute silence. I do praise Him, and I do make certain petitions, but I know that what is most important is that I hear from Him. What He has to say to me is far more important than what I have to say to Him. What He wants is so much more important than what I want. I cannot lose when I wait silently before Him and allow Him to speak to my heart. As you wait in silence before God, there comes a penetration of your soul by the Spirit of God that is deeper and far more eternal than any other touch you could possibly receive. It takes you to a whole new level in Him.

Even while we are active, we can be inactive—if that is an understandable concept. Even while we are fighting a battle, we can be standing before the Lord. So even when we are out running the race, we can be standing still before Him. While we are praying, we can be standing before Him. While we are fighting battles, we can be standing before Him. We can be active and still engaged in communion with the Lord.

This habit of standing before the Lord was so effective for Elijah that it carried him through the final days of his life. Then, when he had left the scene, Elisha, his protégé, demonstrated that he, too, had learned the secret of his mentor's power and wisdom:

> And Elisha said, As the LORD of hosts liveth, before whom I stand…
>
> 2 Kings 3:14 and 5:16

Elisha went on to do twice as many miracles as Elijah had done and to prove God's power to his generation. Never underestimate the power of standing before the Lord. Those who learn to do it will be chosen to become the expression of the Father on earth.

Chapter Four

DEVELOPING GODLY DESIRE

And when the woman saw that the tree was good for food, and that it was pleasant to the eyes, and a tree to be desired to make one wise, she took of the fruit thereof, and did eat, and gave also unto her husband with her; and he did eat.

Genesis 3:6

What happened to Eve that fateful day in Eden was not just an accident. Her reaching forth to first lay her hands on the fruit and then to put it into her mouth and eat of it were all based on her desire to have it. It was this *desire* within Eve (and a subsequent and similar desire within Adam) that caused them both to eat and, thus, to disobey God and sin. If the desire had not been there, they could not have been persuaded to do what they did—under any circumstances whatsoever. Desire, then, is a very strong emotion that we must all learn to deal with on a daily basis.

There are both good desires and bad desires, and some desires are universal. In other words, we are born with them. For instance,

41

when you were still a newborn, your mother did not have to sit you down and explain to you the principles of nursing. No one had to instruct you about how to take milk. You were born with the desire for nourishment, and that desire has, in fact, stayed with you to this day. As you grew, your tastes in food changed, and your eating habits changed accordingly. But that did not alter the fact that you were born with a desire for food.

There is also an inherent desire within a man for the companionship of a woman and a desire within a woman for the companionship of a man. That is why we marry. Marriage is the normal direction for us to take in early adulthood to satisfy desires that were placed in us by the Creator Himself. The problem comes when we take these natural desires and use them in a way that God never intended them to be used.

Look at what happened to Adam and Eve. The tree of the knowledge of good and evil that was located in the Garden of Eden was not planted there by Satan. It was God's tree, and He put it there in the garden for a purpose. Satan wanted Adam and Eve to sin against God, and he came to the conclusion that the only way he could achieve it would be to persuade them to use what God had provided in a wrong way—in a way He never intended. The tactic worked, and this is a tactic that the enemy of our souls is still using against us today. As a result, you and I are often guilty of the sin of Adam and Eve in one way or another.

Spiritual Desire and How to Focus It

There is also inherent in humans a spiritual desire, a desire that causes all people everywhere to worship. Many mistakenly worship objects, people, or false gods. This is another example of taking a desire given by God and using it in a way He never intended.

Clearly there are desires that are motivated by God, and there are desires that are motivated by others. All too often, in the exercise of our growth and natural development, we reach out for what is offered to us by those who have wrong motives.

The advertising world operates on this very principle. The objective of advertising executives is to make you want something you may not have even known existed. Through their ads, these marketers want to stir within you new desires, desires that are, in a great sense, unnatural. These desires were not placed in you by God, but are crafted within you as totally new desires through the use of appealing images and sounds.

It is important, as a human being created in the image of God and with the ability to desire, to learn to focus our desires on God, for He responds to us on the basis of our spiritual desire. And He is not able to respond to some because they lack spiritual desire. The more spiritual desire we have, the more God can do in and through our lives. The Bible uses the metaphor of singleness of eye:

> *The light of the body is the eye: therefore when thine eye is single, thy whole body also is full of light; but when thine eye is evil, thy body also is full of darkness.*
>
> Luke 11:34

We might say it this way: The more we can focus our desire on God, the more He can infuse Himself and His light within us and fill us with Himself. The narrower our desires become (as they, in their narrowness, focus upon God), the greater the opportunity we will have of knowing Him and having His power manifested in us.

Guarding the Gate

The wise King Solomon wrote:

> *For as he [man] thinketh in his heart, so is he.*
>
> Proverbs 23:7

What does that mean? The word translated *"thinketh"* in the original Hebrew is *sha-ad*, meaning *"to gate."* So as a man *"gateth,"* or as a man operates the gate of his heart, so is he, or so he becomes. This is an important principle.

Becoming the Expression of the Father

How the gate to your heart is operated determines your future. It is just that simple. How wide will your gate be swung open? And to what? In how many different directions will you open yourself? The more you open yourself to wrong desires, the more wrong things will be able to enter.

The way you operate the gate to your heart determines your future.

There is a scientific principle at work here. The broader you widen your scope of concentration, the less you can focus on one specific thing, and the "thing" we want to be sure to keep in focus is God Himself. The more you let other interests enter into your life, the less you are able to concentrate on Him and His will for you. Zero in on that spiritual area of your life, and your soul will flourish.

When Jesus warned of avoiding the *"broad"* way (Matthew 7:13), He was saying that we should not open ourselves to every desire, only to godly desire. What would your life be like twenty years from now if you could open yourself more to God's desires and close yourself to all others? In the degree that you learn to control the gate of your heart, that is what you will become.

What an opportunity lies before us all! But how can we take advantage of it? We can do it by exercising our will not to open the gate of our hearts to desires that are not convenient for us as believers. Only we have that authority.

Many, I fear, have not yet realized how powerful this truth is. No one can force you to open yourself to desire—no one. Conversely, no one—not even God—can force you to close the gate to your heart. Again, only you have that authority. And it is your decision about using that God-given authority that will make you what you will ultimately become. What you open your heart to and what you close your heart to will determine the development of your philosophy of life and the way you live out that philosophy. This one thing can affect absolutely everything else about your future.

In this life, you will be touched by many people and many things. You must determine what influence they will have on you. Unfortunately, you were not born in heaven, but in this world. Consequently you will be in constant contact with the world and its power. There is no escaping this fact.

As children, we have no choice about where we will grow up. We all grow up in the world. At an early age we are sent to school, and our classmates are not angels. As a result, as good as our home environment may be, we begin to learn things that angels would never teach us. This has its negative influence upon our thinking and, thus, our total formation.

The Development of Deeply Ingrained Desire

As we continue to live and grow in the world, we usually develop certain worldly or world-like patterns of thinking that constantly dig at our subconsciousness, developing in us certain desires. "If Johnnie has a football, then I have to have a football too." These types of thoughts constantly play upon our hearts and give us no rest day or night. Eventually, we learn that we should work hard in order to "keep up with the Joneses," and we do that by any means possible.

This is just an example of the thinking that becomes so deeply ingrained in us that when we accept Christ and come into His king- dom, we are encumbered with lots of baggage, our old patterns of thinking. How sad for God! When He gets us, we are dragging a thousand things around behind us, and He has them all to deal with. This is why the writer of the book of Hebrew said:

Wherefore seeing we also are compassed about with so great a cloud of witnesses, let us lay aside every weight, and the sin which doth so easily beset us, and let us run with patience the race that is set before us.

Hebrews 12:1

Becoming the Expression of the Father

What was the writer saying? He was saying that we need to narrow our focus in life. But how can God strip us of so many unnatural and ungodly desires and cause our focus to narrow? What a hard job He has! Certain desires have been taking root in us for twenty years or more, and now the Spirit of God has the unenviable task of ridding us of them so that we can focus on the eternal.

Some of us come to God even later in life, and our natural desires have been developing longer. Whatever the case, the sad truth is that many Christians live for years struggling to deal with the inbred natural desires that existed in them when they came to Christ. The Lord is continually dealing with them, and yet they seem incapable of leaving some of their learned behaviors behind.

The Spirit of the Lord is faithful to move upon our hearts and to urge us to lay aside the old ways and to narrow our focus until it is only on Him. It is His desire that we be as narrowly focused as is possible upon this earth. When we can achieve this, we have a head start on others in eternity.

When you enter the life to come you may do so with a foundation already laid that will permit you to be propelled into opportunities that others may never have. Having a narrowed focus will give you a definite advantage that will result in your being brought into positions of responsibility—in this life and in the life to come.

This will not happen because God loves you more than others, but because you have responded to Him and, through determining to operate well the gate to your life, have brought yourself to a place of higher qualification.

First, You Must Be Stripped

This can be your future, but first you must allow the Lord to strip you of the old. And this is a problem. After all, who wants to be stripped? This reluctance often foreshadows resistance.

When we begin our Christian lives, we do so with great confidence. Peter felt that way:

46

Peter answered and said unto him, Though all men shall be offended because of thee, yet will I never be offended...Though I should die with thee, yet will I not deny thee.

Matthew 26:33, 35

There seems to be a lot of Peter in all of us. We have great hopes for ourselves. We will surely become spiritual giants, being rich and full in God, and become so anointed that we can be used mightily in His kingdom. We intend to follow Him "all the way."

We are confident that we can handle situations as they arise, and our Christian lives start out that way—with us in total victory. Some hypocrisy inevitably appears in us, but it is quickly consumed by the fire of the Lord.

We are thrilled when this happens, and as the Lord takes us deeper into His love, other such things are consumed. This process continues...until, at some point, the flames burn more intensely than we feel comfortable with, and we suddenly draw back. Enough has been consumed already, we consider. The fire is getting too hot for comfort.

Tragically, such a drawing back often spells an end to our spiritual growth. It is not that God is unwilling to take us further, but that we are unwilling to go where He wants to take us. After all, we want to exist, and the fire of God seemed to be growing so intense that it was almost life-threatening.

If we had gone further, we wonder, would there be anything left of us? There are certain aspects of our character and culture that we feel are indispensable, so we simply must preserve them. There are things about us we are unwilling to let go of.

When this happens, we may become confused about what exactly is happening. It is simple. We found ourselves agreeable with some of God's initial workings in us, but then, as we saw our favorite desires begin to be subjected to the flames of His love, we drew back. After all, if God requires *this* sacrifice, what might be next? Is there no end to His demands?

47

Becoming the Expression of the Father

When we come to this spiritual impasse, which, again, often spells the end of our spiritual progress, the confidence that we once felt about our spiritual future suddenly takes flight. When this happens, it signifies that we have learned what many men and women before us learned as God drew them nearer and nearer to Himself: We love ourselves much more than we should, much more than we imagined, and we are slow to want to die to self.

Being Willing to Die to Self

As believers in Christ, we are not only required to die to self, but we also are required to do it daily. Paul wrote to the Corinthian believers:

I die daily.

1 Corinthians 15:31

Why *"daily"*? Because it cannot be done in a single day.

God could do it in a day, but He would never have our cooperation. We must be *willing* to die for it to happen. Our surrender is a necessary element in the process. Jesus taught His disciples:

If any man will come after me, let him deny himself, and take up his cross, and follow me. For whosoever will save his life shall lose it: and whosoever will lose his life for my sake shall find it.

Matthew 16:24-25

You are the one who must do it. No one else can do it for you. And you first have to be willing to do it. It will not be forced upon you by the Lord.

What did Jesus mean by *"take up his cross"*? Did He mean that we have to suffer on the cross like He did? No, that has been done, and once was enough. He meant that as He died, we must also die—to self, and we must do it *"daily."*

48

But while God is trying to kill us, we are struggling to cling to life. And as long as we are still moving, His perfect plan for our lives is frustrated.

Dying to self, then, is a lifelong process. Get used to the idea, and submit to it—willingly and joyfully.

Some make remarkable progress in their spiritual lives, only to stop the process at some point and insist on going no further. They eventually come to the conclusion that no further progress is possible. And it isn't...as long as they remain unwilling to continue.

Dying to self is a lifelong process.

Death frightens all of us, just as the consuming fire of God frightens us, and losing control of our lives frightens us. We all have plans for our lives, and we resent it when anyone gets in the way of those plans—even God. The result is that God's hands are tied. He cannot do what He wants to do for us, and it is because He does not have our cooperation.

Our thinking is often warped. We dread words like *sacrifice*, *surrender*, and *dedication*, when these are just pathways to progress. To us, it all sounds like too much loss. In reality, these words represent nothing but gain.

We sometimes justify our lack of progress by saying that, in reality, God has not asked us to do more. In some cases, this may be true. He will not ask of us that which He already knows we are unwilling to give.

Yielding What Is Within Our Power to Yield Right Now

Another reason that our dying to self must be done daily is that we cannot surrender to God that which we do not yet possess. We may say that we surrender our tomorrows, but it is only after we have what tomorrow offers that we know whether we are indeed willing to surrender it. So, in a great sense, it is literally impossible to surrender everything to God at once. We do not yet have it to surrender, and we cannot say truthfully that we are willing to surrender it…unless and until it is actually in our possession. So the key is to surrender what you have today, and let tomorrow present its own challenges.

How can you know what you will do with what God places in your hand tomorrow? You do not yet know what it will be, so how can you surrender it already? You may receive something you never dreamed of receiving, and when the time comes, you might not be willing to surrender it. God may require that you surrender more than you are willing. You just don't know what tomorrow holds.

You cannot give what you do not have, and you cannot know your own mind in a given matter before the moment arrives. Far too often we become so strongly attached to something that we are unable to give it. The Lord knows this, and He will always take it into consideration when He speaks to us. The Scriptures declare:

There hath no temptation [test] taken you but such as is common to man: but God is faithful, who will not suffer you to be tempted [tested] above that ye are able; but will with the temptation [test] also make a way to escape, that ye may be able to bear it.
1 Corinthians 10:13

God is *"faithful,"* and He knows our limitations. He will not ask us to do what we are not able to do. And yielding everything about tomorrow is one of those things that we are not able to do. This, again, is the reason He deals with us on a *"daily"* basis. Release what you are currently able to release, surrender to Him what you are able to surrender, and tomorrow will take care of itself.

If you were not able to surrender everything to God today (and most of us are not), let Him work in you so that you will be willing to surrender more tomorrow. Never be discouraged with your progress, and never stop moving forward. Know that none of us is yet perfect, and determine to continue working toward perfection in the days ahead.

When the Lord deals with you tomorrow about surrendering something to Him, you might well say no, but stay open to Him, continue to love Him, and ask Him to continue changing your heart. Your day of victory will come, and soon you will be living a life of daily victory over your flesh.

Prepare yourself for a life of surrender, for that is what the Christian life is all about. John the Baptist said:

He must increase, but I must decrease.

John 3:30

Allow the Lord to increase in your life and to narrow your focus…until He fills it completely. This is accomplished by surrendering and releasing to Him each thing that He requires as it comes.

Allow the Lord to increase in your life and to narrow your focus…until He fills it completely.

It may occur to you at some point that if you continue to respond to the Lord, as He takes you along His pathway, you won't have much left. Just trust the Lord that He knows what He is doing. You can be sure that He has a wonderful design in mind for you, and although you cannot yet imagine what it will be, as you surrender daily to Him, His glorious plan will slowly emerge.

My Own Initial Resistance to God's Desire for Our Family

When I made that first trip into the Amazon jungle, my purpose had been to see whether I might bring the entire family there. (As I said previously, we were living in the city of Iquitos at the headwaters of the Amazon.) After seeing the situation in that village, I wondered how wise it would be to take the rest of the family there—especially since we had a small baby at the time. "You must be kidding!" I said to myself. "I couldn't bring them into such an unhealthy situation."

Part of the reason everyone was sick in that place was the lack of training in basic sanitation. I had witnessed this firsthand and survived, but I decided that it definitely would not be wise to return there with my wife and children. That was just out of the question. Then something happened that changed my way of thinking.

During one of the last days I was there in the Indian village, I was reading my Spanish Bible. A few of the Indians also spoke Spanish, and one of them, seeing what I was doing, said to me, "God has sent you here to bring us His Word." Those words hit me in the pit of the stomach just as if he had taken his spear and struck me through with it. In that moment, I knew that God had spoken to me.

I had my ideas about whether or not it was wise for our family to go back to serve this primitive tribe, but God had other ideas. He was calling for a sacrifice, for full surrender. And, by His grace, I was able to come to the place of saying yes to Him.

"If You want me to return here with my wife and children," I prayed, "I'll do it. And if they perish, they perish. Their lives will be in Your hands."

That day I had been called upon to make a surrender I had never dreamed I would ever have to make, and I was able to make it. Other sacrifices would follow.

We had experienced many levels of surrender along the way. When the time had come for us to leave our homeland, for instance, Violet and I both found it painful to leave our families behind. We wondered if we would ever see her elderly mother again. Who knew? And we were right; she died while we were on the mission field.

By the time we were on the plane prepared to take off from American soil, leaving so much and so many behind, there was a commitment and a dedication to God sufficient for that day. It would not have been sufficient for what was to come in the days ahead. We would need more. But, as He is known to do, God would continue to work in us, to encourage us in our dedication, and to bring us to a willingness for further surrenders. Each time we took another step forward, it would lead to greater abilities and greater open doors.

As the plane lifted from the runway that day, a powerful score of music, a symphony of God never heard before, played in my soul. The title of it was "This Is the Will of God." It filled my heart with a new joy. When we become willing to make our surrenders and to die our deaths, there is set before us a joy that allows us not only to endure the present sacrifice, but also to make further dedications and surrenders as they become necessary.

Eventually the time arrived when Violet and our small children accompanied me back to that small Indian village (a trip of sixteen days upriver). Over the coming months, the village children, one by one (without exception), contracted malaria. Their little bodies turned yellow, and some of them died. This came in addition to the previous sickness that had continued to plague the area.

Before we had left home, I had asked about any preventative medicines our children might take to keep them from contracting malaria, and I was told that there were none that were safe for children. So what could we do? We refused to keep our children isolated from the other people, as one missionary suggested we should do. How could we minister to the people and remain apart? We had been sent to love them and win them to God. We could not do that by isolating ourselves from them.

We ate with the people, and we ate what they ate. (It was not uncommon for us to see our children eating on a roasted monkey arm.) Our children played with their children in the normal way, quickly adopting the Indian customs of dress and decoration. The people loved them and frequently and fondly caressed their fair skin (because they had never before seen a white child).

Through it all, our children not only never contracted malaria, but they also never so much as suffered a common cold. They enjoyed better health during the time we were among those tribal people than they had when we were living at home in America. We came to the conclusion that the Lord had stretched us so that He could enrich us.

A Refusal to Yield to His Desire Brings Grief

I would not want to contemplate what would have happened if we had chosen to disregard God's desires for our lives. When I was still a student in Bible school, there was a fellow student, a young lady, who had a great missionary call upon her life, and sure enough, many wonderful doors opened to her soon after she graduated. Her parents, however, were so opposed to her doing missionary work that she gave up the idea. Within four years, that girl was dead.

When the Lord strips us, it is with the intention of enriching us, but when we decide to enrich ourselves, the Lord strips us, and this time, there will be no riches. When Jesus said to His disciples, *"For whosoever will save his life shall lose it: and whosoever will lose his life for my sake shall find it"* (Matthew 16:25), He meant it.

Expect God to deal with you about more surrender, and expect Him to do it often in the days and years to come. As you draw nearer to Him, He will burn more and more of you up…until your life is lost in God…until no single desire of your own remains…until He becomes your all. Then there will be no plans but His, no desires but His, and no goal but His.

When this happens, you may feel lost, but in losing yourself, you will find a life that you never dreamed existed. You will find riches that you never knew God had reserved for you.

54

Don't expect it to happen overnight, for it will take time. But it will happen. You can start receiving now, and no doubt you have, but you must also continue so that your spiritual riches can be increased.

Then, when you come to the point that you feel enough of you and your ways have been burned up, or when you come to one of life's most crucial decisions (like whom you will marry), and your desire does not coincide with God's, what will you do? Will you ask Him to consume your own desires, or will you take a step back from Him, lest His fire interfere with what you love most?

If you choose to draw back, what will become of the riches that God has ordained for you? Who will fill the position that was ordained for you from ages past? Will another take your crown, your office, and your riches? Will another be forced to assume what was appointed for you because you have turned your back on it?

Once you have caught a glimpse of the fullness of the wealth, the worth, and the wisdom of the desires of God, you will not even want to touch one of your own desires—let alone fulfill them. You will not even want to look at one of your own, all because of the glory, majesty, and brightness of the desires of God for your life.

Comparing God's desires and your own is like comparing a penny to a million dollars. There simply is no comparison. So which one do you want? The penny? Don't be ridiculous. And yet some people are just that ridiculous when it comes to the things of the spirit realm. They continually reach out for that which is temporal, that which does not last, at the cost of that which is eternal. For this reason, the psalmist admonished:

Delight thyself also in the LORD; and he shall give thee the desires of thine heart.

Psalm 37:4

When your own desires have been consumed by His fire, and His desires are now your desires, then that which you desire

55

Becoming the Expression of the Father

becomes eternal. Those who have taken this step are candidates to become the expression of the Father in the earth.

Chapter Five

RESPECTING THE POWER OF WHAT GOD HAS SAID

And God said....

Genesis 1:3

This powerful phrase is repeated often in Genesis 1, but this first chapter of the Bible is not simply part of the account of Creation; it is much more. It is a revelation of God as Creator and a revelation of the method He uses to create. His method is not one that many might consider "scientific"; it is supernatural. He creates by His word.

The writer of Hebrews would later declare:

Through faith we understand that the worlds were framed by the word of God, so that things which are seen were not made of things which do appear.

Hebrews 11:3

That is exactly how our God has always done it. He simply *"said"* it, and it happened. For example:

Becoming the Expression of the Father

*And **God said**, Let there be light: and **there was light**.*

Genesis 1:3

*And **God said**, Let the waters under the heaven be gathered together unto one place, and let the dry land appear: and **it was so**.*

Genesis 1:9

*And **God said**, Let the earth bring forth grass, the herb yielding
seed, and the fruit tree yielding fruit after his kind, whose seed is
in itself, upon the earth: and **it was so**.*

Genesis 1:11

*And **God said**, Let the earth bring forth the living creature after
his kind, cattle, and creeping thing, and beast of the earth after
his kind: and **it was so**.*

Genesis 1:24

The First Man and His Revelation

After the creation of all other living things, God next made man
(and woman), and He blessed them:

*And God blessed them, and **God said** unto them, Be fruitful, and
multiply, and replenish the earth, and subdue it: and have dominion over the fish of the sea, and over the fowl of the air, and over
every living thing that moveth upon the earth. And God said,
Behold, I have given you every herb bearing seed, which is upon
the face of all the earth, and every tree, in the which is the fruit
of a tree yielding seed; to you it shall be for meat. And to every
beast of the earth, and to every fowl of the air, and to every thing
that creepeth upon the earth, wherein there is life, I have given
every green herb for meat: and **it was so**.*

Genesis 1:28-30

An understanding of God's method of creation is essential to living the life He desires us to live. It was just such an understanding that gave Adam the wherewithal to move successfully toward the purposes of God for his life. I am convinced that before any other revelation came to his heart, this one came. He knew about creation, about the Creator, and about the unique method God employs.

Before God ever approached Adam to establish a personal relationship with him, Adam first had to be invested with this basic revelation of God as Creator and of the method He uses to create. From the beginning, Adam had to know that when God speaks a thing, it happens. This was to be the most important revelation in his life. If he could learn to move in it, it would bring him to a successful conclusion.

Ever since Adam's time, success in living a godly life has been directly related to the intensity of an individual's revelation of the power in the truth *"and God said."* Everything that we need is contained in that one statement. Depending on how this truth grips your heart and with what intensity you embrace it, that is how successful and fulfilled you will be in God's kingdom. That's how important this phrase is.

You will be successful and fulfilled in God's kingdom only to the extent that "and God said" grips your heart and you embrace it.

After Adam learned that things happened when God spoke them into existence, God said to him that he should *"be fruitful, and multiply, and replenish the earth, and subdue it: and have dominion over the fish of the sea, and over the fowl of the air, and over every living thing that moveth upon the earth."* But how was Adam to accomplish all this? Unlike us, he did not seem to wonder. If God had said it, that alone placed it in the realm of possibility. Adam may not have known everything, but he was sure of this one thing. Although he had no idea just how he would obey God's command to its fullest extent, if God had spoken it, then it was God's problem, not his.

Adam's Secret of Success

This was Adam's secret of success. He knew that when God had spoken a thing, the mechanics of it were unimportant. God would do it—somehow. He could not fail.

Adam had not had to wonder about all the details of creation. God had said it and it had happened, and Adam was sure it would be the same this time. His was not to reason out the how and why of things; his was simply to accept the revelation of God and of His method and to move with it.

Since everything that God does is done in the spirit world by the revelation of His word, this should be our main concern, not the mechanics of how things work. The details will take care of themselves. Whatever God speaks to us, we do not have to "sweat the details." That is His job, and He is good at it. If He has spoken it, that is enough. We can move on His word. Jesus said:

Heaven and earth shall pass away, but my words shall not pass away.

Matthew 24:35

He went even further:

For verily I say unto you, Till heaven and earth pass, one jot or one tittle shall in no wise pass from the law, till all be fulfilled.

Matthew 5:18

When God speaks, *"all"* will be *"fulfilled."* What more do we need?

How could Adam have dominion over the high-flying *"fowl of the air"*? He was not worried about it. He just believed God's word.

When God said, *"I have given you every herb bearing seed,"* Adam believed it. He did not need to worry about how it would happen.

The choice is always ours. God does not force us to receive His word reserved for us. He offers it, but we can refuse. Adam was not forced to obey, and neither are we. When we, by choice, bring our lives under the impact of the word of God, then we will be blessed.

The Appearance of Another Voice

Then another voice entered Adam's life. Until that moment, he only knew what God had said, but now he was about to hear another opinion, an opposing viewpoint:

Now the serpent was more subtil than any beast of the field which the LORD God had made. And he said unto the woman, Yea, hath God said, Ye shall not eat of every tree of the garden?

Genesis 3:1

This new voice was both misquoting and contradicting what God had said, and Adam and Eve had the challenge of deciding which one to believe—the serpent or the Creator. The alternative to obedience to God was now portrayed to them as *"good for food,"* *"pleasant to the eyes,"* and *"to be desired to make one wise,"* and Eve was somehow convinced. As we saw in the previous chapter, she *"took of the fruit thereof, and did eat, and gave also unto her husband with her; and he did eat"* (Genesis 3:6).

In one sense, the first man and woman cannot be blamed. After all, they had known only truth, only right, only God. How were they to know that the word of another was not as reliable as His, that it was, in fact, the opposite of the truth? What would be wrong with eating something *"good for food"* and *"pleasant to the eyes"*? And, of course, there certainly could not be anything wrong with something that would *"make one wise."* It all sounded wonderful, so why not go for it? What could possibly be wrong with it?

Becoming the Expression of the Father

The thing that was wrong, of course, was that the serpent was contradicting what God had said. And God was their Friend and Confidant, their Supplier, their Teacher, their All. He had been so good to them. How could they believe another when what this intruder was saying was in direct contradiction to Him whose word had always made things happen for them?

Alas, Adam and Eve made the wrong decision, they ate, and their eyes were opened. In this way, the evil word they had believed and acted upon was fulfilled—in a certain sense:

> *And the eyes of them both were opened, and they knew that they were naked; and they sewed fig leaves together, and made themselves aprons. And they heard the voice of the LORD God walking in the garden in the cool of the day: and Adam and his wife hid themselves from the presence of the LORD God amongst the trees of the garden.*
>
> Genesis 3:7-8

It appears that Adam and Eve became wise the hard way, and, in the process, they became alienated from God. Oh yes, God could have come down like some super policeman and stood before them and forced them to do what He wanted. But He is not like that. He woos us, but then He leaves the decision in our hands. He wants our love, but He cannot force us to love Him.

Jesus' heart broke as He witnessed those who had gone astray from the Father's love in His time on earth. Still He left them to make their own decision. Some of them did right things, but they did them to look good in the eyes of men, not to please God. He spoke of those who did *"alms before men, to be seen of them"* (Matthew 6:1), those who loved *"to pray standing in the synagogues and in the corners of the streets, that they* [might] *be seen of men"* (Matthew 6:5) and of those who disfigured their faces so that others would think they had been fasting (see Matthew 6:16). *"They have their reward"* He said of all those who do such things (Matthew 6:2, 5, 16), but that *"reward"* never included His very best, and it never will. There are blessings that God has determined for certain individuals from the foundation of the world, but they often forfeited those blessings by believing the lies of another.

Jesus loved the men of His day who were like these and offered to cover them as a mother hen covers her chicks, but they refused even the visible and living Son of God (see Matthew 23:37-39). How shocking! As the Word, He was the Creator, and it was apparent to everyone who loved Him and followed His ministry that when He spoke, things happened. Yet, many chose to reject Him.

Yes, God could have placed obstacles in their pathway and prevented them from taking the course they did, but He didn't. He gives us the choice. Then it is up to us what we do with it.

You, too, have a choice. You can go for what the world offers and have your eyes opened by stark reality, or you can choose to believe God and move forward upon His word over your life.

God Continued Speaking and Creating

After the initial Creation was finished, God did not cease to speak. He was still speaking in the book of Exodus. There we find Him speaking to Moses and to the children of Israel in bondage in Egypt:

And the LORD spake unto Moses...

Exodus 6:10, 13; 7:8; 8:1

God not only continued speaking, but He also continued acting, reinforcing and developing the revelation that He was the Creator, that His method of creating was by speaking His word, and that when He spoke, things happened. At the time, the children of Israel were enslaved by the Egyptians, but God prepared them and led them forth in the great Exodus. As always happens, there were other voices that spoke to the escaping Israelites, and as with the serpent and Adam and Eve, these voices spoke in contradiction to what God had been saying. For instance:

And they said unto Moses, Because there were no graves in Egypt, hast thou taken us away to die in the wilderness? wherefore hast

thou dealt thus with us, to carry us forth out of Egypt? Is not this
the word that we did tell thee in Egypt, saying, Let us alone, that
we may serve the Egyptians? For it had been better for us to serve
the Egyptians, than that we should die in the wilderness.

Exodus 14:11-12

These men, of course, had heard the word of God in Egypt, and they had witnessed the plagues sent upon Pharaoh and his people as confirmation of that word. They were eyewitnesses to the fact that when God spoke things happened. Still they chose to believe another voice, that of Satan, God's avowed enemy, and they became his spokesmen.

These men, too, found fulfillment of the word they chose to believe and speak. They did die in the wilderness—just as they had predicted. Be careful what you believe for! You may actually get it.

What God had said was altogether different from the word to which these men gave voice. He told the people to go forward. He would divide the sea before them, and He would destroy Pharaoh and his armies:

And I will get me honour upon Pharaoh, and upon all his host,
upon his chariots, and upon his horsemen. And the Egyptians
shall know that I am the LORD, when I have gotten me honour
upon Pharaoh, upon his chariots, and upon his horsemen.

Exodus 14:17-18

Of course, all that God said came to pass exactly as He had spoken it, and those who had believed it rejoiced in the victory it brought them.

God Spoke and Created Through the Prophets

The word of God operated in this powerful way throughout the history of Israel. Consider, for instance, the case of the prophets.

When Samuel was just a boy, God spoke to him and laid in his young life a foundation for faith in His word:

> *And the LORD said to Samuel, Behold, I will do a thing in Israel, at which both the ears of every one that heareth it shall tingle.*
>
> 1 Samuel 3:11

Often God speaks in an unusual way at the beginning of one's spiritual life in order to establish the revelation of who He is and how He works. This ensures that the person can find his or her spiritual bearings and be founded in the knowledge of "thus saith the Lord." In this way, Samuel learned at quite an early age that what God said produces results.

Elijah learned this same lesson, and he learned it so well that he moved at the word of the Lord:

> *And it came to pass at the time of the offering of the evening sacrifice, that Elijah the prophet came near, and said, LORD God of Abraham, Isaac, and of Israel, let it be known this day that thou art God in Israel, and that I am thy servant, and that I have done all these things at thy word.*
>
> 1 Kings 18:36

Elijah prayed that it might not rain, and it did not rain (see James 5:17). But, before he prayed it, God had spoken it. Then, after God had spoken that it would rain once again, Elijah prayed for rain, and it rained (see verse 18 of James 5). Elijah knew that the word of God was sure and steadfast and that whatever God said would happen. Although there may have been little physical evidence of rain in a time of extended drought, the prophet knew that God's speaking it brought it into the realm of possibility.

As far as God was concerned, it was history before it ever happened. And if you exercise faith in the word of God, what He says can be as good as done for you before there is any physical evidence of it and before anyone else knows that it is even possible.

Becoming the Expression of the Father

Elisha operated under this same principle. The word of the Lord came to him, and as he repeated it, it came to pass. It became *"the saying of Elisha"*:

> *And he went forth unto the spring of the waters, and cast the salt in there, and said, Thus saith the LORD, I have healed these waters; there shall not be from thence any more death or barren land. So the waters were healed unto this day, according to the saying of Elisha which he spake.*
>
> 2 Kings 2:21-22

As these and other powerful prophets moved in the knowledge of what God had spoken, they changed the world around them.

David Believed in the Creative Power of God's Word

The psalms are full of examples of the power of God's word because David was a great believer in its creative power. Here are just a few examples from a single psalm:

> *Wherewithal shall a young man cleanse his way? by taking heed thereto according to thy word.*
>
> Psalm 119:9

> *Thy word have I hid in mine heart, that I might not sin against thee.*
>
> Psalm 119:11

> *Unless thy law had been my delights, I should then have perished in mine affliction.*
>
> Psalm 119:92

> *Through thy precepts I get understanding: therefore I hate every false way.*
>
> Psalm 119:104

Respecting the Power of What God Has Said

Thy word is a lamp unto my feet, and a light unto my path.

Psalm 119:105

God's word becomes the stabilizing and nourishing factor in our lives, moving us, lifting us up, and filling us. This is better than any vitamin supplement. Get a shot in the arm of this. No wonder Elijah could go forty days on the strength of a single meal!

Once God spoke to me, and I went on the strength of it for more than two years. It happened in this way.

Some months before I entered Bible school as a student and for many months afterward, the presence of the Lord was very intense in me. I could neither eat nor sleep on a regular schedule. I did not complain about this; it was most wonderful to me.

Then, quite suddenly, the consciousness of God's presence vanished from within my being, and I was left to wonder what had happened. I thought I must have sinned or that I was even permanently backslidden, although I could not put my finger on any particular point of disobedience that would have caused this. Still, I just knew it had to be there somewhere.

Prayer and Bible study were now meaningless to me, and I was floundering in the dark. God was nowhere to be seen or touched. I struggled on for weeks like this, attempting to break through my darkness, but there was no apparent progress.

I was about to give up when one of my teachers, Walter Beuttler, ministered one Sunday morning in the chapel service on the subject "Walking By Faith, Not By Feeling." That helped me for a couple of weeks, but still there seemed to be no light in my life. The blackness only got worse (if that were possible).

I became more discouraged, and eventually I began thinking: "What's the use? I might as well quit school." Eventually, my mind was made up. I would attend Sunday services one last time, then I would get up very early in the morning on Monday and steal quietly out of the school grounds and go home—never to return again.

Becoming the Expression of the Father

That Sunday morning it was again Walter Beuttler who was ministering. He spoke on "Waiting for God." When the others went to dinner, I went back to my room, having decided to give God one last chance. As the others ate, I would wait for God.

Even as I did this, I had no expectation that things would change. There was now not even a glimmer of hope in my heart. It would not have been right of me not to even give God a chance, but I was sure that nothing would come of it.

I sat at my desk with my arms folded, and informed God: "Here I am." I had no idea where He was at the moment.

"I suppose You know I'm leaving early tomorrow morning," I continued. "If there is anything You would like to say to me before I go, this is Your chance."

He kept me waiting for less than a minute, and then in the pit of my stomach I heard the clear and distinct words of the Spirit: "Isaiah 43."

That was all He said. I had no idea what Isaiah 43 said, and I could not imagine that it could speak to my current dilemma. "I'm in really bad shape," I told the Lord, "and I need something from the New Testament." Then I waited for some New Testament reference to come.

Again, He did not delay. Within seconds, He spoke to me, and it was with the same clarity and distinction. It came as before, in the pit of my stomach, and amazingly it was exactly the same words, "Isaiah 43."

I was a little disappointed that the Lord had not given me a New Testament reference, but I thought it could not hurt to turn to Isaiah 43 to see what it said. Since no verse was give to me, I started to read from the first verse:

But now thus saith the LORD that created thee, O Jacob, and he that formed thee, O Israel, Fear not: for I have redeemed thee, I have called thee by thy name; thou art mine. When thou passest

through the waters, I will be with thee; and through the rivers,
they shall not overflow thee: when thou walkest through the fire,
thou shalt not be burned; neither shall the flame kindle upon
thee. For I am the LORD thy God, the Holy One of Israel, thy
Saviour: I gave Egypt for thy ransom, Ethiopia and Seba for thee.
Since thou wast precious in my sight...

Isaiah 43:1-4

I could read no further for my tears blurred the words. I quickly repented of my distrust and unbelief, and my plan to leave Bible school was forgotten. I had a new light that would see me through the next two years of darkness. There is nothing quite like hearing from God. His word changes everything.

Beginning with Adam and continuing until the present, man has been destined to be brought to the place of perfection, not because he has come to understand everything (no man has yet reached that plane), but because he has loved what God said. And if you have a love—a hunger, an open heart—for what God has said, then He can bring it to pass in your life.

Jesus Lived Out This Principle of Creation

When Jesus came to earth, He illustrated this principle from the very beginning of His ministry. As He walked along the shores of Galilee seeking disciples, He saw Peter. Approaching him, He said, "I'd like to use your boat." After they were out in the water a little, He said to Peter, *"Launch out into the deep, and let down your nets for a draught"* (Luke 5:4).

Peter was skeptical. What did a carpenter know about fishing? It was not even a time when the fish would normally be catchable. And he and some of his men had fished all night the night before and had caught nothing (see verse 5). But something caused Peter not to reject the words of Jesus outright. He had been impressed with the teachings of this Man, so he decided to humor Him. He

69

launched out and cast out one of his nets. It was not full obedience, but it was a start.

Then Peter got the surprise of his life. Something happened that he would never forget. Suddenly, the revelation of the power of the creative word came to him, and it brought him to his knees in confession (see verse 8).

The miraculous catch of fishes astonished not only Peter, but also everyone who was with him that day. Thus was the foundation laid in their lives of the great truth, *"And God said,"* and thus did they begin their life with the greatest Teacher who ever lived.

Jesus would later reveal the secret of the words He spoke. They were His Father's words:

> *Then said Jesus unto them, When ye have lifted up the Son of man, then shall ye know that I am he, and that I do nothing of myself; but as my Father hath taught me, I speak these things. And he that sent me is with me: the Father hath not left me alone; for I do always those things that please him.*
>
> John 8:28-29

This is the reason He could claim that His words would not pass *"till all be fulfilled"* (Matthew 5:18).

Later, Jesus took His disciples in another boat and said to them, *"Let us pass over unto the other side* [of the lake]*"* (Mark 4:35). As they were en route to the other side, a terrible storm arose, and the disciples, despite the fact that several of them were veteran fishermen, felt that their very lives were threatened.

As the winds and waves pounded them and their boat filled with water, Jesus slept in the rear of the boat. Unable to bear it any longer, they finally woke Him up, declaring that they were about to *"perish."* Somehow the words He had spoken and the words they now spoke were at odds. He said that they were going to the other side, but they said they were about to perish. This shows that they had not believed Him. But mercifully the Lord did not allow the disciples to suffer what they had predicted. He stepped in and rescued them from perishing, speaking peace to the storm. And, of course, it obeyed Him. At His word, *"the wind ceased, and there was a great calm"* (Mark 4:39).

The disciples would not have perished. When Jesus says that we are going to the other side, then we are going to the other side—regardless of what happens. When He speaks, it is as good as done. We can count on it. On this occasion, the disciples failed their test, but Jesus helped them anyway—so that their faith would be stronger the next time. How great is His mercy and love!

When God speaks, it is as good as done.

This experience left an indelible impression upon the disciples. Mark recorded:

> *And they feared exceedingly, and said one to another, What manner of man is this, that even the wind and the sea obey him?*
> Mark 4:41

On yet another stormy night on the lake, the disciples were rowing a boat against the wind, alone this time, and suddenly Jesus came toward them walking on the water. What happened that night shows that the lessons He had given them there on the Galilee were taking hold—particularly in the life of Peter. When he saw Jesus, he said, *"Lord, if it be thou, bid me come unto thee on the water"* (Matthew 14:28). By this time, Peter knew that if Jesus said it, it could be done, and he was seeking a word from the Master.

Jesus knew this, so His answer was extremely simple: *"Come"* (verse 29). That was good enough for Peter, and he got out of the boat and began to walk on the water.

Becoming the Expression of the Father

He did well at first...until he noticed how the powerful wind was kicking up waves. Then, what he saw took precedence over what he knew the Lord had said, and he doubted and began to sink.

Jesus' word *"come"* had been spoken with calm and assurance, but suddenly it seemed to Peter that he would surely be drowned. "This is the end of me," he must have been thinking.

Fortunately, Peter did the right thing. He called out to Jesus, and the Master pulled him from the waves.

Sense moving in your soul the quality of the divine, and know that as He moves you on into the revelation of Himself as Creator and of the creative power of His word—through lesson after lesson—His purpose is to move you ever closer to Himself. In time, the power of the word in your life and the might of the God behind that word will overshadow and outshine every difficult situation, so that you can move swiftly and safely through every trial and every affliction, with the word sustaining you. Then you will not fail, and your faith will not fail.

Speaking and Creating Through the Holy Spirit

God did not stop speaking when Jesus went back to heaven. His word kept coming to the early Christians throughout the book of Acts. Now, however, God was speaking through the third Person of the Trinity—the Holy Spirit. God not only spoke through His Spirit, but the Spirit then spoke through men.

On the Day of Pentecost, for example, Peter suddenly had a new boldness and a new wisdom and power. He had gone through the Beautiful Gate of the temple dozens of times before, but one morning soon after Pentecost something proved to be different. He suddenly and unexpectedly turned to a crippled beggar and said to him:

Silver and gold have I none; but such as I have give I thee: In the name of Jesus Christ of Nazareth rise up and walk.

Acts 3:6

And, because what God says always comes to pass, the man got up and not only went walking, but also leaping and praising God.

Throughout the book of Acts, we see God speaking in many different ways, and His word brought results. On one occasion, an angel of the Lord spoke to Philip:

And the angel of the Lord spake unto Philip, saying, Arise, and go toward the south unto the way that goeth down from Jerusalem unto Gaza, which is desert.

Acts 8:26

Philip obeyed this unusual message delivered by an angel, and after journeying for a while, he saw a chariot stopped along the desert road. Approaching it, he saw an apparently wealthy man sitting in it reading. The Spirit spoke to him again:

Then the Spirit said unto Philip, Go near, and join thyself to this chariot.

Acts 8:29

It must have been intimidating for Philip to approach a man of obvious wealth and position, but when the Spirit speaks, there is always fruit. Again, Philip obeyed, and the results were marvelous, affecting the future of Ethiopia and the Gospel there.

God also spoke to the early believers through visions, such as the one Peter had while praying one day on a rooftop in Joppa. He did not understand the vision, but as he thought on it, the Lord showed him what to do:

While Peter thought on the vision, the Spirit said unto him, Behold, three men seek thee. Arise therefore, and get thee down, and go with them, doubting nothing: for I have sent them.

Acts 10:19

Peter undoubtedly would not have gone with these men if he had not received such a word from the Lord; they were Gentiles, and the

73

Jews had no dealings with the Gentiles. Now, however, the vision made sense. In it, he had seen many types of animals considered by his people (the Jews) to be unfit for human consumption, but the voice of the Lord had told him to eat them. This confused him, and he had answered, *"Not so, Lord; for I have never eaten any thing that is common or unclean"* (Acts 10:14). This was repeated three times. Now, he was beginning to understand. The Lord was overruling his own traditions, his own desires, and his own thinking. What men considered to be unclean could be easily cleansed by God.

God was overruling tradition and calling for obedience. "Just do what I say," He was urging. And that was good enough for Peter. Against all that he had been taught, he moved in the word of God so that God could bring forth from that a new creation. The result was the beginning of revival among the Gentiles.

God spoke to the early disciples through prophecy:

And when he was come unto us, he took Paul's girdle, and bound his own hands and feet, and said, Thus saith the Holy Ghost, So shall the Jews at Jerusalem bind the man that owneth this girdle, and shall deliver him into the hands of the Gentiles.

Acts 21:11

Of course, it happened just as Agabus had said it would.

God spoke to the early disciples in many different ways, and He continues to speak today. This pattern continues to the final chapter of the book of Revelation, where we read:

And he said unto me, These sayings are faithful and true: and the Lord God of the holy prophets sent his angel to shew unto his servants the things which must shortly be done.

Revelation 22:6

Believe it and live. God said it, and it shall be so. Those who develop a healthy respect for what God says place themselves in line to become the expression of the Father in the earth.

And God Said

The power of the word of God is mystic in its work and light.

It is seen and heard and touched, but not by earthy ear or sight.

It moves in mystery and majesty to build a kingdom of great work.

It comes to open hungry hearts to live forever in song and mirth.

But first it moves in pain and sorrow, working in dark nights of woe,

For to bring the glorious dawning and "God said," and "it was so."

Charles A. Haun

Becoming the Expression of the Father

Chapter Six

SEEKING TRUE PROSPERITY

This book of the law shall not depart out of thy mouth; but thou shall meditate therein day and night, that thou mayest observe to do according to all that is written therein: for then thou shalt make thy way prosperous, and then thou shalt have good success.

Joshua 1:8

Prosperity is something that interests us all, but it is only after we enter into or realize the former part of this verse that we can have what the latter part promises. We do indeed have the power to make our way *"prosperous"*—but only by bringing our lives under the pattern indicated in the first part of the verse.

The word *prosperity* is commonly understood as meaning having financial plenty, but it means much more than that. It could be translated as "to be in good condition" or "to bring to a successful conclusion." That is what God called Joshua to do with the conquest of Canaan—to bring the conquest to a successful conclusion and to leave the Israelites in a good condition. Joshua was promised that this would be the outcome—if he gave attention to the requirements.

Let us look at some of the biblical keys to prosperity.

The Key of Repentance

The road to prosperity begins with repentance, but please don't stop there.

He that covereth his sins shall not prosper: but whoso confesseth and forsaketh them shall have mercy.

Proverbs 28:13

Repentance signifies a change in direction and must not be limited to a turning away from sin. It includes that meaning, but it goes much further. You see, the word *repent* has neither a good nor a bad connotation. You can repent from good and do evil, just as you can repent from evil and do good. This is why the Bible can speak of God repenting. He was changing the way He dealt with man. This also explains why the Bible says that God does not repent. I am sure that this has seemed contradictory to some. God, in Himself, does not change, but He does change in His particular dealings with us and with mankind as a whole.

Prosperity comes when we execute a change of direction within our lives, and that change of direction does not come in a single day or with a single act of contrition. Please never think that your repenting days are over just because you have gone to an altar and prayed and become a Christian. At that point, your repenting is just beginning. Turning your life around is not just the act of one day, but a process that must be carried out over time. When you repent of your sins and invite Jesus to come into your heart, you have simply made a good beginning, nothing more.

Periodically God will approach us and offer us something new, and receiving that something new will again require a change of direction in our life patterns. He is constantly redirecting our lives, and we must be willing to make the necessary adjustments. This is where the Pharisees hit a snag in their spiritual lives. They were unwilling to change when Jesus came on the scene to introduce them to new horizons, and many of us are just as resistant to change.

It is easy to become set in your ways, become accustomed to your life as it is, and not want to welcome any radical readjustment. The result is rebellion, an unwillingness to repent, a resistance to change. When this is the case, God has a difficult time with us. He tries to get us to change, and we resist.

Those who are serious about giving their lives to full-time service for the Lord will be required to make radical changes often. In order for God to use us, we need to change our way of thinking, our way of acting, and our way of approaching life in general. Students who are entering Bible schools have a lot of repenting to do. Many rebel against this necessity and soon forsake their training. This often spells the end of their calling, for those who are unwilling to change can forget full-time service for the Lord.

In reality, most people dislike change. We dislike anything that disrupts the current rut our lives are in, and it is not uncommon for men and women of all walks of life to resist the changes God wants to make in them.

The fact that repentance is necessary to a successful Christian life, not only as an initial step away from sin, but also as a continuing method of spiritual growth, explains why many never go far in God. They are like the children of Israel who grew so accustomed to their wandering in the wilderness that they had difficulty adjusting to the blessings of a land flowing with milk and honey.

Never become so rigid in anything that God cannot change you. If you are unwilling to change, there is not much that God can do with you. You may have started your race well, but there is no way that He can bring it to a successful conclusion unless you are willing to change along the way.

Becoming the Expression of the Father

In each period of revival that sweeps the earth, massive changes come. Those who are unwilling to move with the Spirit of God, unwilling to change their methods, are bypassed, and others are raised up in their stead. We wonder why God uses young people or those with limited Christian experience. Often it is simply because the young and inexperienced are willing to do things His way, while others are not.

The various branches of the Pentecostal movement came into being precisely because men had become so rooted and grounded in their religious traditions that they could not (or would not) change, and God wanted to move by His Spirit in a new way. Periodically, when new moves of His Spirit come, invariably some of those who were used in the last movement refuse to move on, cling to the past, and are left behind.

Whether you are eighteen or eighty-eight, remain pliable in God's hands, and He will bring you into ever greater perfection.

The Key of Obedience

It should be obvious to us that obedience is one of the necessary elements of prosperity—spiritual and otherwise. After all, Moses said it clearly throughout Deuteronomy: that we *"observe to do"* everything written in God's Word. Obedience and change go hand in hand. If there is no obedience, how can there be change? If God is calling you to change, how can you do that unless you become obedient to Him?

David, when instructing the people on necessary preparations for the rebuilding of the temple in Jerusalem, said:

> *Then shalt thou prosper, if thou takest heed to fulfill the statutes and judgments which the LORD charged Moses with concerning Israel: be strong, and of good courage; dread not, nor be dismayed.*
> 1 Chronicles 22:13

"Then..." "Then shalt thou prosper." Then you will be in good condition. *Then* you can move on to a proper conclusion in your life.

Today, we have the idea that we can be successful only when we achieve our life's objectives, but the Scriptures teach us to concentrate on obedience to God's objectives instead. Many of our personal objectives in life are not very spiritual, and some of them are not even scriptural. Exchange them for God's objectives, and you cannot go wrong.

Our destiny is in God, and our future depends upon Him. That being true, trust Him that He knows how to get us where we should be going (where He wants us to go). Relax and obey Him, and things will go better for you.

What are your goals in life? What are your objectives? Are they God-inspired? If not, you are in trouble before you start. If you want your life to be brought to a successful conclusion here on this earth, you have no choice but to trust Him and obey. Your objectives must be His objectives, and you must work to bring them to fulfillment.

An alarming number of Christians seem to have no goals in life at all. They are just waiting for Jesus to come. But He has admonished us:

Occupy till I come.

Luke 19:13

You have an assigned work to do, so you had better know what it is, and then you had better get busy doing it. Don't be satisfied to pass through life tossed about like a wave of the sea. Get direction for your life and move in that direction.

If you are not sure where you are going, how will you know when you get there? Know your purpose in life, know the direction you are taking, know your God-given objectives, and then get busy in the Word of God to see how you can accomplish it all.

There is no substitute for obedience to the dictates of the Scriptures. Study them, meditate on them, and then obey them.

Becoming the Expression of the Father

All direction must come from the Word of God. The problem in our modern world is often that our busyness keeps us from being able to search the Word. Wise people learn to lay aside time-wasting things that have no spiritual benefit—or very little spiritual benefit—in order to get into the Word, see what is written there for them, and learn to relate it to their daily lives. This brings true prosperity.

Once you have found a way to spend time in the Word of God, then begin to move under the dynamics of it. Put little confidence in what people tell you, but put every confidence in what you learn from God's Word. People are sometimes wrong, but God is never wrong. People sometimes fail, but God never does.

Put little confidence in what people tell you, but put every confidence in what you learn from God's Word.

Once you have discovered your direction and purpose in life, then seek to conform, to obey. That is a guaranteed way to bring your life to a successful conclusion.

Don't be content just to make it into heaven. Seek an abundant entrance, a full one. Seek to live your life with as full an understanding as possible, so that when any door is opened to you, you can take advantage of it. Seek to receive all of life's benefits at any given moment. This is true prosperity.

The foundation that has been laid in your life to this point has the purpose of preparing you for the doors God will open for you today and tomorrow. If God is dealing with you today it is because He plans to open greater doors to you tomorrow. Don't fail Him. Be obedient at every step, and that will ensure your continued development.

The Key of Believing

Another key to the successful conclusion to your life is faith in God and faith in His Word. Just as you have faith in Him, you must have faith in His Word. He has chosen to make it the expression of Himself. He has invested it with His power and life. If you do not believe what He has said, how will you obey it? How can you conform to His purposes for your life?

When the children of Israel were threatened by the Moabites and Ammonites in the time of King Jehoshaphat, they sought God for an answer and found it:

And they rose early in the morning, and went forth into the wilderness of Tekoa: and as they went forth, Jehoshaphat stood and said, Hear me, O Judah, and ye inhabitants of Jerusalem; Believe in the LORD your God, so shall ye be established; believe his prophets, so shall ye prosper.

2 Chronicles 20:20

"Believe." It sounds so simple, but it is so very powerful. Just believe, have faith, and the victory will come.

Can we expect the Word of God to make an impact on our world if we do not believe it? Can we expect to be blessed by God if we don't believe Him? Faith is a necessary requirement:

But without faith it is impossible to please him: for he that cometh to God must believe that he is, and that he is a rewarder of them that diligently seek him.

Hebrews 11:6

Much has been written on faith, so let's move on.

The Key of Seeking God and Depending on Him

Those who seek God find Him, and those who find Him find prosperity—in every sense of the word. But something interesting happened to young King Uzziah that should serve as a warning to us all:

> *And he sought God in the days of Zechariah, who had under-standing in the visions of God: and as long as he sought the LORD, God made him to prosper....But when he was strong, his heart was lifted up to his destruction: for he transgressed against the LORD his God, and went into the temple of the LORD to burn incense upon the altar of incense.*
>
> 2 Chronicles 26:5, 16

It is easy to seek the Lord when we are in great need, but when we, like this young king, are feeling strong, we often feel no need of the Lord. This all-too-common attitude often spells the downfall of formerly powerful believers.

The truth is that we need the Lord more when we are strong than we do when we are weak. We may not think so, but it is true nevertheless. Those who are strong have a tendency toward pride. They get *"lifted up,"* and that is a very dangerous state to be in. It takes more wisdom to walk through this life when we are strong than it does when we are weak. The stronger you become, the more strength you need to maintain it. So, in a sense, those who are weak are strong, and those who are strong are weak. Those who are weak are protected, and those who are strong are vulnerable. It seems contradictory, but that's the way it is.

When we are strong, we lose our sense of desperately needing God, and we feel self-sufficient. It is then that we cease to depend entirely on the Lord. Oh, please, guard against this evil. The moment you cease to depend totally upon God, your life is in grave danger.

The moment you cease to depend totally upon God, your life is in grave danger.

There is no way you can have prosperity on your own. There is no way you can bring your life to a successful conclusion on your own. There is no way you can bring things into a good condition on your own. You must depend upon God for it.

Why has God made this to be so? Because if we could live our lives without Him, we would. And that would cut us off from fellowship with the Creator. He has designed us so that we cannot prosper apart from Him. His great love forbids it.

The Key of Choosing the Winning Side

Life is a struggle between good and evil, light and darkness, God and Satan—and one side must fail. Both cannot succeed. Just be sure that you are on the winning side. God said through Isaiah:

> *No weapon that is formed against thee shall prosper; and every tongue that shall rise against thee in judgment thou shalt condemn. This is the heritage of the servants of the LORD, and their righteousness is of me, saith the LORD.*
>
> Isaiah 54:17

The passage speaks of a battle with the use of weapons, and someone has to fail. God said that if we are *"the servants of the LORD,"* failure would always be on the other side, not ours.

As Joshua moved into the Promised Land, he encountered many enemies. If he was to be prosperous and bring to a successful conclusion the conquest of the land, there would have to be many failures among the forces that opposed him. Our enemies must fail if we are to succeed. There cannot be success with us and with our enemies at the same time. One side must fail, and since we don't want to fail, we must be sure that we are on the winning side.

We know what the enemy desires for us:

> *The thief cometh not, but for to steal, and to kill, and to destroy.*
>
> John 10:10

Becoming the Expression of the Father

If we are to prosper, these evil desires of our enemy must fail. If not, our end will be death and destruction. If the enemy is successful in his plans, then we will never be successful. So, the enemy must fail, and he will—if we stay on the right side. Jesus declared it:

Upon this rock I will build my church; and the gates of hell shall not prevail against it.

Matthew 16:18

In order to ensure the failure of his enemies and of their weapons formed against him, Joshua had to go into the land in God's way. He had to be open to a change of direction. He had to obey. He had to seek the Lord and depend on Him, and he had to make sure he was on the right team. If he did this, success would come.

And success did come—first at Jericho and then in other battles. But what happened at Ai is a very good example of what happens when we fail to continually seek God and to do things His way. Because the former cities had been conquered with such ease, Joshua became overconfident and failed to inquire of the Lord about the next battle. At Ai, his forces were soundly defeated, and he was left mourning his losses.

This became an oft-repeated pattern with God's people in the Promised Land. When they sought Him and marched out to battle against their enemies with Him by their sides, they were invincible. When they grew careless and overconfident and acted on their own accord, they were unexpectedly handed stinging defeats.

There is a certainty that enemies will attack us, but the outcome of those attacks depends entirely on us. We can choose to be on the winning side—by doing things God's way.

The Key of Using Failure As a Servant

All of us fail at some point, and learning to handle that failure is another of the keys that can ensure our prosperity. For instance, in that sad case of the prodigal son, at least he woke up one day and realized his error. It may have taken his eating the food provided for pigs, but suddenly he realized that he had failed—in every way— and he turned his heart toward home.

There are two ways to look at this story. We can see the terrible waste and loss of a life thrown away for a time, or we can see the positive side—a son returning to his father's house, which he now realizes he should not have left in the first place. The father chose to take this view (as does our heavenly Father) and welcomed his prodigal son home. The brother (the one who had done everything right) was not nearly as glad to see his sibling. That is the difference between how God looks at failure and how men see it.

Failure often has the benefit of getting us back under the wings of our heavenly Father. It causes us to return to a dependency on Him. When we can no longer depend on others, we are forced to do what we should have done all along. And God is happy about that— whatever brought it about.

Our God knew how to deal with the Israelites in the wilderness:

And he humbled thee, and suffered thee to hunger, and fed thee with manna, which thou knewest not, neither did thy fathers know; that he might make thee know that man doth not live by bread only, but by every word that proceedeth out of the mouth of the LORD doth man live.

Deuteronomy 8:3

Failure has a benefit. So, when you have failed, just get up and start praising God. Just get back under His wing. Just get reconnected to His supply.

If God allows failure in your life, there is a reason for it. He has a purpose. Run to Him. Cling to Him, and everything will be all right.

When everything you have been depending on suddenly slips out from under you, and you find yourself hanging by a thread, that is not easy. But trust God, and don't be discouraged. He has allowed this particular set of circumstances to come your way. Return to your dependency on Him, and prosperity will return to you.

As we know, even Peter failed. Jesus told him that he would be so strong that he could strengthen his brothers, but he suddenly found himself flat on his face in failure. Still, all was not lost. The Lord meant it when He said:

I will never leave thee, nor forsake thee.

Hebrews 13:5

He never leaves us when we are down. Peter was able to make failure his servant and to return to a place of success in God. He overcame his failure and went on to become a truly great apostle. If you have never failed, you are not like the rest of us. Most of us have experienced many failures. The secret is to get back up, realize who your Source of strength is, and keep on walking.

Business people often fail, and some allow their failure to destroy them. Others become stronger through their failures. They learn from their mistakes and go on to do better the next time. Failure is never pleasant, but if we allow it to serve us rather than destroy us, it can be a great blessing in disguise.

When the prodigal son woke up very hungry one day, and when the Israelites hungered in the wilderness, it did not mean that God did not love them. Just the opposite; it meant that He did, and He was drawing them to Himself. When things are not going well in your life, don't be discouraged. Just draw closer to God, and things will turn around for you too.

When you have lost your job and the last of your money has been spent, don't be discouraged. Draw closer to the Father. Let Him become your all in all. When inflation is running rampant in your area and goods are suddenly in short supply, don't despair. God is still rich. Praise the Lord for every failure and know that it brings you back to His heart and away from sin and selfish living.

Just as Joshua's failure at Ai put him back on the right road, some failures are necessary to put us back into proper alignment with God so that we can again prosper.

The Key of Avoiding Presumption

For many years the children of Israel waited on the other side of the Jordan, unable to go in and take the land that had been promised to them. Joshua, one of the spies who were sent into the land to assess the situation, had returned with this report:

If the LORD delight in us, then he will bring us unto this land, and give it us; a land which floweth with milk and honey.

Numbers 14:8

But, as we know, the majority of the spies did not agree with the report (because of the giants in the land), and consequently the people had not yet been obedient to God. This angered the Lord, and He threatened to give all the land to the descendants of the spies who had believed. Finally, He spoke to the people:

Tomorrow turn you, and get you into the wilderness by the way of the Red sea.

Numbers 14:25

God wanted His people to have the land, but they refused, saying that they preferred to go back to Egypt or to die in the wilderness. Now, He told them to go back to the wilderness, and suddenly they decided that they wanted to go in and possess the land. Why was it that they never wanted to do what God told them to do?

A rebellious group decided to take action on their own:

And they rose up early in the morning, and gat them up into the top of the mountain, saying, Lo, we be here, and will go up unto the place which the LORD hath promised....

Numbers 14:40

Becoming the Expression of the Father

None of the priests accompanied this group of rebels, and the ark of the covenant remained in the camp. Moses also refused to go with them. And it was because they were "way off base." What they were saying sounded logical, but what they were doing was not. It may have seemed to some that they were finally claiming the promises of God, but they were certainly not doing it His way.

"Move out," the order came, "with or without God's help." But this venture was doomed from the start. Prosperity comes only in God, no other way.

Moses warned the group not to do this thing, but they refused to listen. Instead, they scorned him and were ready to stone him. They had had difficulty accepting his leadership from the start. Had he brought them out in the wilderness to kill them there? Was he perhaps mentally ill? One moment he wanted them to go into the land, and the next he was warning them not to go. What was wrong with Moses anyway?

Of course, they would not listen to him:

But they presumed to go up unto the hill top....Then the Amalekites came down, and the Canaanites which dwelt in that hill, and smote them, and discomfited them, even unto Hormah.
Numbers 14:44-45

What a sad ending to this story! Presumption is a very dangerous thing. Don't ever entertain it. Move in God, never in presumption. The end of presumption is always disastrous. As you learn the keys to prosperity, your life will be blessed—spiritually and financially—and others will clearly see the hand of God upon you and yours. Those who choose this way are themselves chosen to become the expression of the Father in the earth.

Chapter Seven

RECEIVING THE TRUE WISDOM

Then thou shalt make thy way prosperous, and then thou shalt have good success.

Joshua 1:8

We often use the terms *prosperity* and *success* interchangeably, but here the meanings of the two are quite different. The original word translated here as "success" has a very specific connotation, showing that God's idea of success is quite different from our own. The word means understanding or wisdom, so it refers to spiritual success, spiritual prosperity. Nothing could be more important, and God said so Himself:

*Therefore my people are gone into captivity, **because they have no knowledge**: and their honourable men are famished, and their multitude dried up with thirst.*

Isaiah 5:13

91

Becoming the Expression of the Father

Jesus confirmed this truth when He said:

And ye shall know the truth, and the truth shall make you free.
John 8:32

When Jesus made this statement, He was not talking to sinners. He was, in fact, speaking to His own disciples. As believers, success and failure are determined by our willingness to do what is necessary to achieve spiritual understanding.

To a large degree, the things that we must do to have this spiritual success are the same as those we outlined in the previous chapter that lead us to prosperity. I will not repeat what has already been said, but there are a few points I would like to add.

Repentance Is Again Required

As with prosperity, success requires repentance on our part, a changing of directions. The prophet Daniel noted:

As it is written in the law of Moses, all this evil is come upon us: yet made we not our prayer before the LORD our God, that we might turn from our iniquities, and understand thy truth.
Daniel 9:13

There can be no spiritual understanding as long as a person refuses to leave a particular area of iniquity. Saints and sinners alike must change in this regard.

Peter was concerned about the lack of growth in first-century believers, and he wrote to them:

As newborn babes, desire the sincere milk of the word, that ye may grow thereby.
1 Peter 2:2

This command was attached to a previous one that is important to its understanding:

Wherefore laying aside all malice, and all guile, and hypocrisies, and envies, and all evil speakings.

1 Peter 2:1

Milk will benefit us...if we can lay aside things that hinder growth. If we refuse to lay aside such things, normal growth becomes impossible.

The Corinthian believers had some serious issues to deal with if they were to grow in Christ. These issues included such things as division and strife. Even the original disciples of Jesus argued among themselves about who would be the greatest among them in the kingdom. Jesus had to say to them, *"Are ye also yet without understanding?"* (Matthew 15:16) This was not to say that the disciples were ignorant, but that they constantly needed new understanding as they moved from one spiritual level to another.

A lack of spiritual understanding, then, can be the result of an unwillingness to learn, an unwillingness to lay aside things that hinder growth, or an unwillingness to change. And carnal Christians (those who are unwilling to change) are a dime a dozen. This explains why God does not come to the rescue of all those who claim the promise of 3 John 2:

Beloved, I wish above all things that thou mayest prosper and be in health, even as thy soul prospereth.

No wonder we have so many sick and poor Christians! Prosperity and health come to us in the same measure as the growth of our spiritual understanding. When we make no effort to do the right thing spiritually, how can we expect anything from God? We have tied His hand of blessing. If we go where we should not go and do what we should not do, then God has to deal with us and bring us forcefully back into line so that we can be blessed. In short, if we are unwilling to change, then God has to change us by force, or we risk great loss.

God's Method of Dealing With Us

The Hebrew word translated into English as "repentance" is also sometimes translated as "comfort." Even then the concept of change is present. To comfort someone is to move that person from one area to another—from discomfort to comfort. This is what David meant when he sang:

Thy rod and thy staff they comfort me.

Psalm 23:4

If you have ever experienced God's using the rod (and most of us have), it never seems to be for *comfort*. We know it as "the rod of correction." But such a rod does serve to change us, and that is what the psalmist wanted to say.

If you are going the wrong way, you need correction; and if it takes a rod to achieve that, then so be it. The process may seem anything but comforting, but the end result is indeed comforting. Correction gets you back on the right pathway. Correction brings you back to soundness and wellness, and it accomplishes that task quickly. Believe me, the results of going further astray would be much more painful than the temporary sting of the rod.

When God chastens us, it is not out of anger but out of love:

For whom the Lord loveth he chasteneth, and scourgeth every son whom he receiveth. If ye endure chastening, God dealeth with you as with sons; for what son is he whom the father chasteneth not? But if ye be without chastisement, whereof all are partakers, then are ye bastards, and not sons.

Hebrews 12:6-8

This is why the Bible can say that God's rod comforts us. Parents, therefore, are admonished:

Chasten thy son while there is hope, and let not thy soul spare for his crying.

Proverbs 19:18

Withhold not correction from the child: for if thou beatest him with the rod, he shall not die. Thou shalt beat him with the rod, and shalt deliver his soul from hell.

Proverbs 23:13-14

It may not seem like it at the time, but disciplinary action can save a child—and it can save you too. It is discomfiting at the moment (we all agree on that point), but it is applied so that you can be comforted in the end.

The Hebrew word here translated as "staff" is also translated as "support." This particular staff is one that you lean on for support, one that aids you as you are walking. We all need that. The Lord cannot take you where He wants you to go (including *"through the valley of the shadow of death"*) unless you have proper support. You cannot survive without it.

None of us likes to go through hard places, especially not *"the valley of the shadow of death."* We fear the evil there. But David was able to face this valley because he had support. The rod and the staff kept him in line and helped him to survive.

It is interesting to note the timing of the Lord's rebuke of His disciples. For instance, He did not rebuke Peter when he tried to walk on water and began to sink. Instead, He reached out to support the floundering disciple. It was only after He had Peter safely in His arms again that He said to Him, *"O thou of little faith"* (Matthew 14:31). What a nice way to be rebuked!

The comfort and support of the Lord will bring you safely through *"the valley of the shadow of death."* Then it will keep you during the great banquet in the presence of your enemies, and it will keep you when you are *"beside the still waters."* The ultimate goal is always to know the Lord more fully, and we come to know Him through all the situations He allows to develop in our lives each day—even those that seem painful at the time.

--- ▤◆▤ ---

The ultimate goal is always to know the Lord more fully.

--- ▤◆▤ ---

Through it all, David said, *"I will fear no evil,"* and you can make that same determination. Be willing and ready for whatever comes your way.

Whatever you do, don't fear change, don't fear where repentance will take you, and don't ever fear what God will bring to your life. He has your very best interests at heart.

Providing God With a Platform

Since we know that what God is doing in our lives is for our good, we should embrace it joyfully and be obedient to Him in all things. Daniel purposed in his heart that he would flow with God's plan for his life:

But Daniel purposed in his heart that he would not defile himself....
Daniel 1:8

This young prophet was determined not to resist, but to move under the impact of the ways of God. He did not have to struggle to obey; he wanted to obey. He wanted to move in that heavenly realm.

The majority of the other Hebrew captives in Babylon fell in love with the king's meat and wine and gloried in being able to partake of them. After all, they reasoned, they were captives, so they had to go along with the program. It did not take much to convince them of this necessity.

But Daniel refused to do so. He knew something the others did not know: by remaining faithful to God, he could change things around him. And he did.

Daniel was able to convince his captors to excuse him and three of his companions from the regimen—at least on a trial basis. They would be proven for a short while (ten days). The results of this test were quite amazing:

> *And at the end of ten days their countenances appeared fairer and fatter in flesh than all the children which did eat the portion of the king's meat....As for these four children, God gave them knowledge and skill in all learning and wisdom: and Daniel had understanding in all visions and dreams.*
>
> Daniel 1:15, 17

How did this happen? Could all this have been the result of a ten-day diet? It seems very unlikely. God just poured blessings down upon His sons as a reward for their willingness to be different. The same knowledge and wisdom that they received were available to others of the captives, but they were not willing to deny their flesh and refrain from defiling themselves in order to receive it.

It is always easier to float with the stream than to battle the currents. But just floating with the prevailing currents cannot be considered success. Success is found in obedience when your situation seems practically impossible—even when everyone else seems to be going the other way.

Even dead fish can float along with the current, but do you want to be found in company with them? When you hear the voice of the Spirit of God saying, "This is the way," insist on walking in it—regardless of what others do. That is real success, for it lays a foundation upon which God can work.

Daniel experienced great miracles because he provided God with a platform upon which He could respond. Because the prophet honored God's laws, God was able to respond to him. Because God had found four Hebrew boys who would obey Him, He was able to show Himself strong on their behalf.

Becoming the Expression of the Father

There were probably thousands of Jewish captives in all, but among them God found just these four whom He could honor because they honored Him. In the same way, when Jesus came to earth, there were probably tens of thousands who were touched by His ministry. Still, out of those, He ended up with only one hundred and twenty in the upper room. God has always worked through a small remnant of people, those who have determined in their hearts to walk with Him. This small group provides Him with fertile ground in which to work, a platform upon which He can build success.

King Saul disobeyed God, and this rebellious act knocked all the foundations out from under his leadership. God had chosen him, but now He could not sustain him on the throne of Israel or deliver to him his rightful inheritance.

In the same way, Judas, one of the original twelve disciples, destroyed the foundations of his leadership position and could not come into the inheritance of which the Lord had spoken to him. He would have eventually sat upon one of twelve thrones judging the twelve tribes of Israel. But it would never happen, not because God changed His mind, but because Judas destroyed the foundations that supported his blessing. God could not bless him and make him successful, as much as He wanted to do it.

Daniel and his three friends prospered (succeeded) so much that they provoked jealousy in others, and their enemies conspired to have them put to death—Daniel in the lions' den, and the other three in a fiery furnace. But these threats did not deter them. They knew that God was able to deliver them, and if He chose not to (for some reason), they still would not agree to bow down to other gods or to stop praying to the true and living God. They were determined to serve Him—even if it meant a death sentence.

The earlier decision to not defile themselves with the king's meat and drink had been a prelude to this larger challenge. Now, their very lives were at stake. The fact that Daniel survived the lions' den must have given the other three courage to believe that they could survive the fiery furnace—or anything else to which their enemies wanted to subject them. The pressure must have been great for them to save themselves and make the necessary compromises, but they refused.

The death of these men for their faith would not have been anything new. Believers in every generation have died for what they believed. In the early centuries after Christ, many died by crucifixion and being fed to the lions. Is there victory in such a death? Can that be considered success? Oh, yes, these men and women were successful.

If you want to know God and to have His understanding and wisdom, you must be ready to go His way—whatever that happens to mean at the moment.

Spiritual Desire and the Ministry

Spiritual understanding is not achieved without great desire on our part. In Nehemiah's day, the people gathered because they had a great desire to understand God's ways:

And on the second day were gathered together the chief of the fathers of all the people, the priests, and the Levites unto Ezra the scribe, even to understand the words of the law.

Nehemiah 8:13

If God's house (the physical temple), His church (the people), His Word, and His ministers mean little to us, then we will not go far in God. He has placed it all here for our benefit. If we fail to appreciate these things and to take advantage of them, we become the losers, and the wisdom they afford us is lost.

These men of Nehemiah's time were important men, chiefs of the fathers, priests and Levites, and yet they took time to seek God and His ways. They knew how to order their priorities. I am sure that it was inconvenient for some of them, but when you have a desire to do

God's will, nothing can deter you. They were determined to live a life of dependence upon God, and we must do the same.

We must determine to live a life of dependence upon God.

If you are called to be a shepherd of God's people, an even heavier weight of responsibility falls on you. The prophet Jeremiah was angry with slothful shepherds who failed to seek wisdom from on high:

> *For the pastors are become brutish, and have not sought the Lord: therefore they shall not prosper, and all their flocks shall be scattered.*
>
> Jeremiah 10:21

Pastors are responsible for the flock, and how will they feed their sheep if they themselves have not first been fed? Where will they get the needed food? The disciples participated in the miraculous feeding of the five thousand, but they were not the source of the food. They only distributed it. Those of us who are responsible to feed others must ourselves eat well at the Master's table. We may then assimilate what we have been offered and offer it to others. We ourselves have nothing to offer.

Attaining to wisdom and understanding—especially the type of wisdom and understanding that allows a person to minister to others—does not come in a day, a week, or a month. It requires years of feeding. I prayed about some matters for years before they were opened to my understanding. Seeking God for His wisdom is not a one-time activity. It is only a continual seeking that brings us into spiritual maturity and leadership.

Pastors who fail to seek the Lord cannot prosper themselves, and therefore they cannot help others to prosper. Instead, *"their flocks shall be scattered."* I have seen it happen. Sheep require a lot of attention, a lot of feeding, and a lot of watering. Pastoring is not a job for lazy people.

When you put corn out for the chickens, they come back the next time. If you fail to feed them, they will go elsewhere. Well-fed sheep are happy and healthy, and they have no reason to wander away. But sheep cannot be content with your pleasing personality. They will not be happy with mere human enthusiasm. Seek God for nourishment with which to feed your flock, and depend upon Him to nourish you and yours. Nothing else will suffice.

Coming Short of the Glory

Looking back to Eden again, what was the sin of Adam and Eve that brought such destruction upon the entire human race? If was, of course, a failure to believe God and, instead, believing what the serpent (God's enemy) had said. It also was abandoning their fellowship with God and choosing another. But it was much more than that. They were trying to exist on their own without God's help, looking to a source other than Him, and thus failing to depend on Him and His wisdom.

When the Lord first saw them after the fall, after they had eaten of the tree of knowledge of good and evil, He asked them: *"Who told thee that thou wast naked?"* (Genesis 3:11) In other words, "To whom were you talking? Where did you get this information?" They had sought knowledge and understanding, but they had sought it in the wrong place. God wants to tell us what we need to know. After all, He knows better than anyone else what is good and what is evil.

As a result of their rebellion, Adam and Eve never realized the glory that God had originally ordained for them. This failure passed to all mankind:

Becoming the Expression of the Father

For all have sinned, and come short of the glory of God.

Romans 3:23

The two parts of this statement are not unrelated. The first causes the second. But what is this sin that has caused us to come short of the glory of God?

This verse might be translated "All have missed the mark, or purpose (the word *sin* literally means to miss what is aimed for), and therefore they have come short of the glory of God." What is the mark that has been missed? It is the perfect will of God, and missing it causes us to come short of His glory. Men come short of the glory of God because they act in a manner of their own choosing, whether it agrees with God's desire or not.

The Second Adam, Jesus, came to restore mankind to the glory intended for the first Adam. As Jesus moved about the earth, the Father's approval was evidenced upon His life, and we were destined for that same glory. This little-appreciated truth is emphasized in Paul's letters to the Thessalonians:

That ye would walk worthy of God, who hath called you unto his kingdom and glory.

1 Thessalonians 2:12

Whereunto he called you by our gospel, to the obtaining of the glory of our Lord Jesus Christ.

2 Thessalonians 2:14

We are called to obtain the glory of the Father, and when we *"come short"* of it, He is disappointed. He is glory, and we, as His bride, are to become one with Him. This is accomplished by the Spirit working in our lives, moving through the Word, correcting us, teaching us, and bringing us into the fullness of the Father's will. We cannot live in the carnal realm, as Adam and Eve chose to do, and prosper spiritually. Our lives must be lived in the spirit. As Nehemiah noted:

> *Thou gavest also thy good spirit to instruct them.*
>
> Nehemiah 9:20

The instruction of the Spirit brings us to spiritual success and prosperity. Meditate upon this instruction, and you can lay claim to the promise:

> *And he shall be like a tree planted by the rivers of water, that bringeth forth his fruit in his season; his leaf also shall not wither; and whatsoever he doeth shall prosper.*
>
> Psalm 1:3

When does it happen? It happens when we choose to live under the influence of the eternal wisdom of God. This looses the hand of God in favor over our lives. Those who choose this way are candidates to become the expression of the Father in the earth.

Becoming the Expression of the Father

Chapter Eight

UNDERSTANDING AGAPE LOVE

The first of all the commandments is, Hear, O Israel; The Lord our God is one Lord: and thou shalt love the Lord thy God with all thy heart, and with all thy soul, and with all thy mind, and with all thy strength: this is the first commandment. And the second is like, namely this, Thou shalt love thy neighbour as thyself. There is none other commandment greater than these.

Mark 12:29-31

For years I could not preach on the subject of agape love because what I had been taught and what I saw around me did not seem to line up with what I was reading in the Scriptures. I was confused, and until I understood this subject better I felt that I had no business trying to teach it to others. Then one day I seemed to stumble upon an understanding of the term that not only opened it up to me personally but also allowed me to help others with it.

Agape love is defined as a dedication to the well-being of another. That seems to be straightforward enough, but how can we be dedicated to the well-being of our neighbors? How can we love others with such intensity?

Before we can answer that, let us take a closer look at the strange concept called agape.

The Strange Concept of Agape

Agape is a very strange concept, and our various uses of the English word *love* only complicate our understanding of it. If I were in charge of the English language, I would throw out this *love* word. It is too confusing. Too often we have no idea what a person is talking about when he says *love.*

Is the person talking about love from God, the emotional link between siblings, sex between animals in the field, what a married couple does in bed together—or perhaps something in between? We don't know. These scenarios are all described as *love,* and that is simply crazy.

The Greeks had at least three words to describe what we call love. One of them was *eros.* This term covered animal instinct and some of our strongest feelings (not only in the physical context, but also emotionally). *Eros* is the root of our English word *erotic.*

Then we have the Greek word *phileo,* which can be described as a fondness, such as a friend might experience, or with someone you genuinely like, or as the love between siblings. Philadelphia, the city of brotherly love, is made up of this Greek word and the Greek word for city.

Finally, we have *agape,* the divine love. Although it is so very different from the other two, it is translated into English by the same word—*love.* In reality, there are worlds of difference between these concepts.

I don't like to think of *agape* as love (in the English language) at all, but, because of the lack of a better term, I don't really know what to call it. I have come to call it simply agape, for I have never found a word that I could use to translate it properly.

Agape is a marvelous force that moves from God toward us and then from us toward Him and toward others. It makes choices, and then it is faithful to the choices it has made (faithful, that is, to the object of the choice, or the person to be loved).

If I make a choice for Jesus through agape moving in my heart, then I will be faithful to Him—regardless of the consequences. If I were to be hauled away and cast to the lions, I would still remain faithful to Jesus. Circumstances never change agape.

Peter's Phileo Was Not Enough

Just before His arrest in the Garden of Gethsemane, Jesus said to His disciples:

All ye shall be offended because of me this night: for it is written, I will smite the shepherd, and the sheep of the flock shall be scattered abroad.

Matthew 26:31

Peter was sure that this would never happen to him. He responded:

Though all men shall be offended because of thee, yet will I never be offended.

Matthew 26:33

Of course all the others said the same thing. After all, they would have looked bad if they had not. But let's focus on Peter here. He had made a decision and a commitment, but on what was that decision and that commitment based?

After the resurrection, Jesus took occasion to remind Peter of his words:

Becoming the Expression of the Father

So when they had dined, Jesus saith to Simon Peter, Simon, son of Jonas, lovest thou me more than these [do you agape Me more than these other disciples do]? He [Peter] saith unto him, Yea, Lord; thou knowest that I love thee [I phileo You; I am fond of You]. He saith unto him, Feed my lambs.

John 21:15

In the few short days that had passed since Peter made his promise in Gethsemane, he had come to understand the basis of his own motives. He had made a promise to Jesus never to forsake Him, and he thought he meant it, but he had not been able to keep his promise. This showed that he was not exactly where he thought he was in his spiritual experience.

Jesus brought Peter's words back to him again, and again Peter answered in the same way:

He saith to him again the second time, Simon, son of Jonas, lovest thou me [so, you agape Me]? He [Peter] saith unto him, Yea, Lord; thou knowest that I love thee [I phileo You, or I am very fond of You]. He saith unto him, Feed my sheep.

John 21:16

Jesus had known what was in Peter's heart all along, and He had warned that the disciple would indeed be offended. More specifically, He had warned Peter:

Verily I say unto thee, That this night, before the cock crow, thou shalt deny me thrice.

Matthew 26:34

Again, Peter was sure that this would not happen, and he promised (out of his *phileo*, his fondness for Jesus) that he would never deny Him. His commitment was moving and sweet, but it was not enough. When the moment of test came, he was unable to keep his commitment. It had not gone deep enough. A mere friendship was not enough to risk dying for.

◄═◆═►

Agape provides a firm foundation for relationship.

◄═◆═►

Peter needed agape. Agape would hold him steady in his commitment to the Lord. In the same way, our relationship to God must be built on a foundation that is sure and unchanging. Some element must tie us to Him and keep us tied to Him no matter what—and that element is agape.

Divorcing Love From Feelings

In its simplest form, agape love is a decision, not an emotion. This explains how we can love sinners. Jesus was their friend, and I am too—through my God-given agape, love divorced from human emotion.

Whether we like it or not, we are all saddled with certain emotions, and we have to learn to deal with them. But we cannot allow our emotions to dictate the way we relate to people; we must let the principles of the Spirit and the Word of God direct and lead us in these all-important matters. Agape is not affected by the emotions. It is something totally apart from our natural feelings.

Even though Jesus said love was the very first commandment, the love He described is impossible to have without its being divorced from emotion. This is because none of us feels good toward absolutely everybody. That's all there is to it. Not only do we not like absolutely every living person, but we also do not like every living Christian. We may not have anything in particular against certain people, but their character just rubs us the wrong way, or we don't "hit it off" with them the way we do with others. That is just human nature.

Becoming the Expression of the Father

The truth is that even God does not like everybody. There are some people whom He actually hates. At the same time, He loves everyone (with agape). That sounds like a contradiction, but it is not.

When Jesus taught us to love our enemies (not just those who were once enemies, but those who are still enemies), He certainly could not have meant that we had to feel good about them and enjoy spending time with them. Such people grate against our natural emotions—and for good reason. They have something against us and are out to get us for whatever reason, or, perhaps, for no reason at all. Still, Jesus said that we should love them. That has to be done apart from natural emotions.

If we do not like someone, how can we show that person love? Is it a matter of forcing ourselves to love him whether we want to or not? The short answer is yes. Agape comes out of your will rather than your emotions, and you can make a conscious decision that you will love a person and then do it—even if your emotions tell you something very different. Even if you don't feel like treating the person decently, you can still do it.

How Do You Get Agape?

"Well," you may say, "this agape sounds wonderful, but how do I get it?" This is an important question. Does agape come to us when we are born again? Does it come to us through a vision or revelation? Do we get it when a pastor lays hands on us?

You may be surprised to learn that you already have agape. We all do. Even the Pharisees had it:

Woe unto you, Pharisees! for ye love [agapeo] the uppermost seats in the synagogues, and greetings in the markets.

Luke 11:43

For they loved [the same word is used] *the praise of men more than the praise of God.*

John 12:43

110

The Pharisees already had agape; they just made decisions that focused it in the wrong direction. They decided where to concentrate their God-given love, and it was not toward God or even others. Some people love themselves, and they become a god unto themselves. You and I must make a conscious decision first to concentrate our affections on God and then to develop a genuine concern for our fellow man. Then, through discipline, we must follow through with our commitment. But how is that done?

Loving Your Neighbor As Yourself

Jesus called us to love our neighbors as ourselves, and this unselfish love for one another is not something that we have a choice in. This command demands that we change, that we be willing to forsake self-centeredness and to make a conscious decision to care about the welfare of others. When we genuinely love one another, our decisions are no longer based on our personal well-being but on a concern for the well-being of others. This was the totality of the direction for Jesus' life and ministry on earth:

> ...having loved his own which were in the world, he loved them unto the end.
>
> John 13:1

Jesus refused to live for Himself and, instead, lived for others. The core of His message to His followers in what we have come to call the Lord's Supper was that it was all *"for you"*:

> And he took bread, and gave thanks, and brake it, and gave unto them, saying, This is my body which is given **for you**: this do in remembrance of me. Likewise also the cup after supper, saying, This cup is the new testament in my blood, which is shed **for you**.
>
> Luke 22:19-20

It was all *for you*. His lived His life and died for those who would accept Him. His body would be broken for them. His blood would be shed for them. And He was able to do it because His decision was made in godly love—agape.

Jesus willingly gave His life; it was not taken from Him. The Scriptures make this very clear. And this decision was not forced upon Him, either. It was His own. It was what He wanted to do. Now, let us love others as Jesus loved us.

It is much easier to love God than it is to love people because He is so perfect, and they are so imperfect. But love cannot be reserved for God. If we love Him, we will indeed love others also:

> *If a man say, I love God, and hateth his brother, he is a liar: for he that loveth not his brother whom he hath seen, how can he love God whom he hath not seen?*
>
> 1 John 4:20

It is always cheap to say, *"I love God."* Anyone can say it, and who is to say differently? The proof is in the test our Lord has set forth. Simply parroting the words, "I love you," accomplishes nothing. There certainly is nothing wrong with expressing love in words, but it is never enough.

Love in Deeds, Not in Words Only

Our love to anyone and to everyone should be demonstrated, not just spoken. As John wrote:

> *My little children, let us not love in word, neither in tongue; but in deed and in truth.*
>
> 1 John 3:18

Don't just tell someone you love them; show them. Many times I have said while preaching this truth, "If you love someone, shine their shoes." Once, when I was preaching in Michigan, a man came to me after the service and told me a story that bears this out.

One day a brother from one of the local churches came to visit him and told him that he had come because he loved him.

"Is that so?" the man asked.

"It is," he was assured.

"Well, then, I have a well out there that hasn't produced water in some three years," the man answered rather sarcastically. "If you love me, come and help me dig a new one."

He was sure he would hear no more from this man of "love," so he was quite surprised the next morning when the brother, with two others in tow, all showed up early to help him dig his well. He was not able to resist that kind of love.

Agape is more than words.

Words are cheap. We must love *"in deed and in truth."* Our words must be a genuine expression from the heart that produces a corresponding action. True love, then, cannot be hidden. It becomes visible, or tangible.

Jesus showed us that works need to be seen, not just talked about:

> *Let your light so shine before men, that they may see your good works, and glorify your Father which is in heaven.*
>
> Matthew 5:16

The Tests of Our Love

There are several tests of love recorded in the Scriptures. For instance, Jesus said to His disciples:

> *If ye love me, keep my commandments.*
>
> John 14:15

Becoming the Expression of the Father

These words were written in the present indicative tense, not the imperative, as they appear in this King James English translation. Literally, His words meant: "If you love Me, you *will* keep My commandments." And why will love compel us to do that? Because it is agape, that secret weapon we all need to exercise more often.

Another test of our love for Him is how willing we are to give of our earthly substance to Him and to His work:

Every man according as he purposeth in his heart, so let him give; not grudgingly, or of necessity: for God loveth a cheerful giver.

2 Corinthians 9:7

It would be better to keep our money than to give it to God *"grudgingly."* He responds with agape when He finds *"a cheerful giver."* We must love Him with all of our souls and be motivated to give to His work without regret.

Another test of our love is similar—how much we cling to the *"things that are in the world":*

Love not the world, neither the things that are in the world. If any man love the world, the love of the Father is not in him. For all that is in the world, the lust of the flesh, and the lust of the eyes, and the pride of life, is not of the Father, but is of the world. And the world passeth away, and the lust thereof: but he that doeth the will of God abideth for ever.

1 John 2:15-17

As we have seen, those who love things will eventually suffer great loss. When speaking of the fall of the great city of Babylon in Revelation, the Scriptures reveal the end of the finery she enjoyed:

And the fruits that thy soul lusted after are departed from thee, and all things which were dainty and goodly are departed from thee, and thou shalt find them no more at all.

Revelation 18:14

These *"things"* were not bad in and of themselves. They were *"dainty"* and *"goodly,"* but they had now come to an end, as will all things. Don't get too attached to anything down here. Let agape focus your attention in the right direction. Hold the things of earth lightly, for they are just that, earthly, and therefore temporary:

> *While we look not at the things which are seen, but at the things which are not seen: for the things which are seen are temporal; but the things which are not seen are eternal.*
>
> 2 Corinthians 4:18

Use the things that come to your hands, but never become overly attached to them. Become more attached to God, and allow your soulish appetites to become tempered. If we love the things of this world too much, then agape is not in us.

Love itself became a test of discipleship and sincerity:

> *A new commandment I give unto you, That ye love one another; as I have loved you, that ye also love one another. By this shall all men know that ye are my disciples, if ye have love one to another.*
>
> John 13:34-35

Love God with all your mind, with agape as your unmovable foundation, and you will not make selfish and self-centered decisions. This is how men will know that you are one of His.

It Is Agape That Holds a Marriage Together

This word *agape* is used in the Scriptures even in regard to the need for a husband to love his wife:

> *Husbands, love [agapeo] your wives, even as Christ also loved [agapeos] the church, and gave himself for it.*
>
> Ephesians 5:25

115

Becoming the Expression of the Father

The responsibility of a husband to his wife has nothing to do with how he feels at the moment. It is completely divorced from emotion. Whatever she may have done to offend him recently, he is still called upon to love (agape) her anyway.

The decision a man takes in this regard must not be for his own pleasure but for the well-being of his wife. What a great responsibility! If this guideline is followed, the honeymoon will never end.

An old Dutch proverb says, "Kissing wears out, but cooking never does." I would like to talk to the man who originated that saying, for he has a lot to learn. The honeymoon should never be over for those who love God and know how to appropriate His agape love toward others.

A good husband holds his wife as his objective, and her well-being becomes his interest. His every decision is based upon her needs as agape moves through him toward her. If we had more agape at work today, we would have much less divorce and unfaithfulness in marriage.

Agape Is the Foundation of Our Faith

For in Jesus Christ neither circumcision availeth any thing, nor uncircumcision; but faith which worketh by love.

Galatians 5:6

In order for faith to work, we must have the foundation of love. Ask yourself today, "Can I help somebody? How can I reach out to others? How can I give out what God has given to me so that others may be blessed?" Every time you go to church, go with the intention of blessing someone, and you will be blessed even more:

The liberal soul shall be made fat: and he that watereth shall be watered also himself.

Proverbs 11:25

Do everything in agape:

For, brethren, ye have been called unto liberty; only use not liberty for an occasion to the flesh, but by love serve one another.

Galatians 5:13

...forbearing one another in love.

Ephesians 4:2

...maketh increase of the body unto the edifying of itself in love.

Ephesians 4:16

And walk in love, as Christ also hath loved us, and hath given himself for us as an offering and a sacrifice to God for sweet-smelling savour.

Ephesians 5:2

Promises for Those Who Love With Agape

There are many biblical promises to those who love with agape. Here are just a few:

And we know that all things work together for good to them that love God, to them who are the called according to his purpose.

Romans 8:28

Eye hath not seen, nor ear heard, neither have entered into the heart of man, the things which God hath prepared for them that love him.

1 Corinthians 2:9

...every one that loveth is born of God, and knoweth God.

1 John 4:7

Becoming the Expression of the Father

Blessed is the man that endureth temptation: for when he is tried, he shall receive the crown of life, which the Lord hath promised to them that love him.

James 1:12

Is There Hope for Us?

It all sounds so easy on paper, but still many of us struggle to love. Is there any hope for us? The Scriptures seem to give us some:

And the Lord direct your hearts into the love of God....

2 Thessalonians 3:5

When you see things breaking down in your life and you know that there is no longer a constant faithfulness to be found in you (toward God or one another), don't ignore it or run from it. Bring that failure to the Lord and surrender it to Him, asking Him to direct your heart into the love of God. Ask God to work in you and to get you moving in the direction He wants—away from self and toward Him and others.

If you will do this, I believe you will be surprised at the Lord's attitude toward you. He will not despise your failure, and He will not turn His back on you. He will receive you with open arms, and He will hear your cry and respond to the desire of your heart.

Agape originated in His heart:

For God so loved the world, that he gave his only begotten Son, that whosoever believeth in him should not perish, but have everlasting life.

John 3:16

I am convinced that it was God's intention to transfer agape to us at creation, but the fall left man in a pitiful state. God loved the world, John wrote, but he went on to record:

118

And this is the condemnation, that light is come into the world, and men loved darkness rather than light, because their deeds were evil.

John 3:19

But our God is a God of restoration, and He is able to restore us. It does not matter in what condition He finds us. You may be a wreck, messed up, unloving, uncaring, and unfaithful, but in your weakness His strength can be made perfect. Those who are willing to love as He loves are candidates to become the expression of the Father in the earth.

Becoming the Expression of the Father

Chapter Nine

LEARNING PATIENT WAITING

I waited patiently for the LORD; and he inclined unto me, and heard my cry. He brought me up also out of an horrible pit, out of the miry clay, and set my feet upon a rock, and established my goings. And he hath put a new song in my mouth, even praise unto our God: many shall see it, and fear, and shall trust in the LORD. Blessed is that man that maketh the LORD his trust, and respecteth not the proud, nor such as turn aside to lies.

Psalm 40:1-4

"*I waited patiently.*" Patient waiting is not one of the things most of us do well these days. In fact, it is perhaps the most difficult task we could be called upon to do. We would much rather be busy, for we find waiting to be boring. We can wait patiently for just so long, and after that any waiting we do is no longer done with patience.

Many of us have experienced waiting in a doctor's office for an appointment. After half an hour or so of waiting, the wait seems to

Becoming the Expression of the Father

become intolerable, and our patience grows thin. We are also not very patient when it comes to waiting in supermarket checkout lines or in traffic on our highways. When it comes to patient waiting, we have a problem.

What Is Patient Waiting, and Where Do We Wait?

Before we go any further, let me clarify that when I speak of waiting on God, I am not suggesting waiting for His coming. I am talking about waiting for *Him*.

The Hebrew word used here in Psalm 40 conveys the meaning of a very long wait. David was saying, "I waited and waited." His waiting went on for quite a long while. That is fairly typical of the patient waiting the Lord calls us to.

Hosea and the psalmist both saw this patient waiting as being without interruption, continual, *"all the day"*:

Therefore turn thou to thy God: keep mercy and judgment, and wait on thy God continually.

Hosea 12:6

Yea, let none that wait on thee be ashamed: let them be ashamed which transgress without cause. Shew me thy ways, O LORD; teach me thy paths. Lead me in thy truth, and teach me: for thou art the God of my salvation; on thee do I wait all the day.

Psalm 25:3-5

But if we wait continually, how can we get anything done? As we saw with standing, waiting does not imply total inaction. We can wait while we do other things. What God expects of us is that we develop a waiting attitude toward Him, and He chooses the place of our waiting to achieve maximum effect.

In the case of Psalm 40, the place of waiting was a *"horrible pit,"* an uncomfortable place, to say the least. When we are called to such a place for waiting, we tend to focus on our discomfort and forget the

Lord, who is the reason for our waiting in the first place. Also our discomfort with the place of waiting often causes us to cut our waiting period short, or, at the very least, not to wait with patience.

Waiting is just plain hard, so why does the Lord require it of us? It is because patience is not a part of our character and must be developed in us. Uncomfortable situations are perfect for such development. Paul wrote:

> *And not only so, but we glory in tribulations also: knowing that tribulation worketh patience* [patient waiting].
>
> Romans 5:3

The Greek word that is translated here as "patience" is actually composed of two words meaning "under" and "dwell." We are brought into situations under which we are forced to dwell for a time, and the purpose is so that we might learn to trust God and to wait patiently on Him. And, despite the fact that situations under which we are asked to dwell are uncomfortable for us, the Lord is looking for a good attitude from us. We might say that He loves a patient waiter.

Patient Waiting Teaches Us to Welcome Tribulation

Tribulation is not something that we usually welcome, but we should. It works patience in us. It teaches us patient waiting. Job also knew what it was to be in a horrible pit:

> *When I looked for good, then evil came unto me: and when I waited for light, there came darkness.*
>
> Job 30:26

Jeremiah had a similar experience:

> *Give glory to the LORD your God, before he cause darkness, and before your feet stumble upon the dark mountains, and, while ye*

look for light, he turn it into the shadow of death, and make it gross darkness.

Jeremiah 13:16

Experiences such as these can be quite distressing. Often we do not immediately understand just why God allows them. Most of us do not even dare to recognize that such experiences *are* from God. We pray, and we pray some more for them to be lifted, and we moan and groan before the Lord about our situation. In all of this, we are not at all relaxed about the way things stand, and we are usually not patiently waiting for something good to come from the darkness that suddenly seems to surround us. In fact, as I said, our only prayer is usually to escape from the circumstances—whatever they happen to be. We don't even consider for a moment that God wants us to wait patiently *in* that condition.

Then after a while we discover that we can do nothing else but wait, and we do wait—but not very patiently. Instead, we wait anxiously. We cannot wait to get out of that miry clay, out of that horrible pit, out of that dark situation. As a result, it takes some time for us to develop the quality of waiting that God requires of us. We must stop and remind ourselves of the specific reasons God has permitted this thing—that we might develop qualities that we cannot get in any other way.

Patient Waiting Always Has a Purpose

We never wait patiently for the sake of patiently waiting. It is not that God is somehow blessed by the fact that we are willing to wait for Him. We are the benefactors in this, not God. He has a specific purpose in everything that He does in us, and His goal is *our* perfection. He is already perfect. If we can learn to wait upon Him, we will become more like Him.

Patient waiting serves the greater purpose of teaching you to trust God, and without that trust you can never become close to Him and become His expression in the earth. Once He has built enough trust into you, then you can successfully run the race that is set before you, fighting the good fight, having developed the qualities that will enable you to bring forth the harvest He has destined for your life.

—◆—

The purpose of waiting is learning trust.

—◆—

In every productive garden there is a lot of work to be done, and the soil of your life is no different. Your soil is being prepared for maximum output, not only in this life, but throughout eternity as well. Let the Lord work on you while you wait upon Him.

In Jeremiah's day, the people complained of having to sit still and of having to suffer inconveniences, including having to drink *"water of gall,"* meaning bitterness:

> *Why do we sit still? assemble yourselves, and let us enter into the defenced cities, and let us be silent there: for the LORD our God hath put us to silence, and given us water of gall to drink, because we have sinned against the LORD. We looked for peace, but no good came; and for a time of health, and behold trouble!*
>
> Jeremiah 8:14-15

The impatience of these people is palpable. *"Why do we sit still?"* You have probably said the same thing many times. They were waiting, but not patiently. Eventually they became so discontented with the need to wait that they decided to go elsewhere.

"Let's get out of here" is a common refrain. Anyplace else seems more convenient than the place God has set us. Because we have not learned to trust Him fully, we are looking for a way to escape to other (and more favorable, we hope) circumstances. Surely another place would offer more security. But would it? Can any place be more secure than the place God has set us? Definitely not!

There is something very important for us to see here in these verses. Satan always makes us believe that the trials we are currently

125

enduring are a result of our sins *("because we have sinned against the* LORD*").* But those who know the Lord know His mercy and grace. He readily and easily forgives iniquity. Those who do not believe this lack revelation. No, the patient waiting God has called us to has nothing to do with our sins. It is not a punishment. It has many benefits.

Patient Waiting Destroys Preconceived Ideas

Oh that thou wouldest rend the heavens, that thou wouldest come down, that the mountains might flow down at thy presence, as when the melting fire burneth, the fire causeth the waters to boil, to make thy name known to thine adversaries, that the nations may tremble at thy presence! When thou didst terrible things which we looked not for, thou camest down, the mountains flowed down at thy presence.

Isaiah 64:1-3

We all have our preconceived ideas of what God should do and how He should do it, but we forget that He knows perfectly well how to do all things. When you learn to wait upon Him and His way, you begin to forget your preconceived ideas. It may be only natural for us to expect God to do things as He has done before, but He prefers to surprise us.

Some years ago in a church I was pastoring, I was preaching on the six verses of Isaiah 12 that speak of the Spirit of God coming into the midst of the people, when a strange thing began to happen. I noticed that a small cloud had begun to form at the back righthand corner of the sanctuary ceiling. I thought in passing how curious this was, but I kept on preaching. Occasionally I would glance that way, and each time I could see that the cloud was growing in size. Eventually it covered the entire ceiling of the church, and, as I continued to preach, it moved downward toward the people.

By now I was in awe at what was happening. The cloud was literally sitting on the heads of the people. Then, suddenly, the place exploded with jubilation. People jumped from their seats and made such a joyful noise that I could no longer hear myself preach.

My attention was drawn to one elderly gentleman. He was so sedate and proper that he never displayed any emotion in the services. He always sat at the back of the church and never uttered a word. Now I saw tears flowing down his cheeks, his hands were uplifted to the Lord, and he was worshiping. Others were responding to the strange presence of God in our midst in their own way. It was a sovereign move of God.

I had never seen a cloud like that in a church service and did not know that things like that could even happen. Of course I wanted God to do that same thing over and over again in every service after that (and I would love to see Him do it again these days), but He chooses to display His glory among us in other ways.

As you wait before God, let Him loose you from every preconception so that He can demonstrate His love to you as it pleases Him at the moment. Don't get boxed in with your thinking. God is not limited by your preconceptions. Wait before Him for His delightful surprises.

God will never conform to your preconception. His will is to do *"great and mighty things"* that you do not know:

> *Call unto me, and I will answer thee, and shew thee great and mighty things, which thou knowest not.*
> Jeremiah 33:3

It is impossible for God to respond to our preconceived ideas, for He refuses to be confined by our limited thinking. Instead, He does things we have never thought of, never heard of, and never seen:

> *For since the beginning of the world men have not heard, nor perceived by the ear, neither hath the eye seen, O God, beside thee, what he hath prepared for him that waiteth for him.*
> Isaiah 64:4

Becoming the Expression of the Father

So you are waiting for God, and you don't know what you are waiting for, and you do it because that is the way He works. As you free Him from your preconceptions, He will begin to do *"a new thing"* in your life:

> *Behold, I will do a new thing; now it shall spring forth; shall ye not know it?...*
>
> Isaiah 43:19

Refraining from preconceptions means more than just letting God do what He wants to do in the way He wants to do it. It also means not trying to figure out how you should respond in a given situation. You are allowing God to be God.

Patient Waiting Allows God to Act in His Time

Usually, if we pray about some matter, we wait only a short time before deciding to take things into our own hands. This is sad because God knows how to handle life's situations a lot better than we ever could. Patient waiting on Him means that you give Him permission to handle a situation—in His own way and in His own time—and you refrain from taking action on your own. He may show you something to do, but that is a different matter.

> *Wait on the LORD, and keep his way, and he shall exalt thee to inherit the land: when the wicked are cut off, thou shalt see it.*
>
> Psalm 37:34

In God there is always a proper timing, and you must be willing to wait patiently for Him to move. This was proven so powerfully in the life of Jesus. For instance, few of us would have wanted to put up with Satan's presence or his temptations even for a moment. Yet, when Satan approached Jesus in the wilderness (see Matthew 4), Jesus did not immediately "send him packing." He realized that the temptation must run its course. He must be tried. Therefore He tolerated Satan's presence for a time.

It was only in verse 10 of that chapter, after several other conversations had already taken place, that Jesus told Satan to get out. Understanding the Father's timing, He knew exactly when to say, *"Get thee hence."* You and I would have said it much earlier, but the timing was important.

We always want an answer from God **now**, but His timing is perfect. And He always does things on His time—not ours.

We often wonder why God delays, and, as we have seen, Satan assures us that it is because we have sinned. But God knows that we must be subjected to certain situations for a certain amount of time—not too much and not too little. We could never know those things.

This is the reason that we often say to Satan, "Get thee hence," and nothing happens. It is not time yet. When God's time is perfect, there can be no argument. When we say, "Get thee hence" in God's time, Satan immediately obeys.

Learn to wait patiently for God in obedience, and learn to march to His time. These two lessons will bring great productivity to your life. For instance, if I do the exact same thing I did ten years ago, I may be blessed and I may not. It is a question of timing.

David had this experience. Moses numbered the people and was excused, but when David did the exact same thing, it was counted for him as sin. Aside from timing, what the two men did was not significantly different. Do things when God wants them done, and your actions will always be blessed.

This is why you cannot do today what God has intended for you five years from now. The timing is not right. Visions must await their time of realization.

What we are presently seeing in the church is just the tip of the iceberg. There is much more beneath the surface that has not yet been revealed. If we can just become clay in the Father's hands and wait before Him in obedience, He will reveal it all in His time.

Patient Waiting Enables Us to Focus on Him

When we talk about waiting for God (waiting on God, or waiting upon God, as some say), we often make the mistake of thinking that we are waiting for something *from* Him. We are waiting on *Him*, not on something *from* Him. Let Him remain the focal point of your waiting. He alone can be your all in all.

Just as God's focus is on you, your focus must be on Him. Those who lose their focus go astray. God's desire is to make you a proper habitation for Himself, and your desire must be to make Him your habitation.

Notice what Isaiah said:

Yea, in the way of thy judgments, O LORD, have we waited for thee; the desire of our soul is to thy name, and to the remembrance of thee. With my soul have I desired thee in the night; yea, with my spirit within me will I seek thee early: for when thy judgments are in the earth, the inhabitants of the world will learn righteousness.

Isaiah 26:8-9

*"We waited **for thee**; the desire of our soul is **to thy name**, and to the remembrance **of thee**. With my soul have I desired **thee**... with my spirit within me will I seek **thee**...when **thy** judgments are in the earth, the inhabitants ...will learn."*

Isaiah did not pray, "God, what can You do for me?" He waited for God. Most of us are guilty of beginning our relationship with the Lord based on what He does or can do for us. Because of this, we seem to be in it for what we can get.

And what we get is not to be demeaned: We get free salvation, free deliverance, free baptism, and free healing. But if we are not careful, we will soon develop a mind-set that says, "What else can I get from God?" What we want to get is *Him*; we are not in this relationship to take Him for all He is worth, but to know Him better. The Christian life is not just about what we can get from God. There is another side to it. It takes two to form this relationship. So what can God get from you?

Although most of us begin our Christian lives with this immature view of our relationship with God, there comes a time when He attempts to wean us from this limited thinking. He takes us from the bottle, and, of course, we cry and don't understand what is happening to us or why. We run here and there trying to get advice because this is a very difficult time for us. What is happening should be simple for us to understand: God is weaning us from things and drawing us to Himself.

The reason for our waiting is simple: God is weaning us from things and drawing us to Himself.

Dr. Simpson, the founder of the Christian and Missionary Alliance Church, said, "Once it was the blessing, and now it is the Lord. Once it was what I could take Him for, and now I love Him—just Him alone."

Don't be alarmed by this language. This is a definite step up, and you will not lose anything in the process. God still loves you and will continue to bless you—more than ever, in fact. The difference is that you will no longer focus on the blessing but on the Blesser. In Him, you will find all that you need. If you remain focused on daily life, you will miss many wonderful discoveries in God.

You are not waiting for help, for sunshine, for money, for health. You are waiting for God. He has now become the desire of your soul. We love Him—regardless of whether He has done anything for us or not. And we will serve Him—regardless of whether He does anything else for us in the future.

131

Becoming the Expression of the Father

There are those who serve the Lord only so that they can escape hell and get into heaven. Although going to heaven is a worthy goal, that is not why we serve the Lord. We serve Him because He is God, because He is the Creator of the universe, because He is Master of all. Heaven is a wonderful place, and we all should desire to go there, but please serve God for who He is, not for entrance into heaven.

If getting into heaven is your objective in life, you are probably not a very effective Christian. If you love God and obey Him, heaven is your destiny. You will go there whether you have focused on it or not. It is not something that you have to think a lot about. It just happens.

And what will happen to those who are hung up on heaven when it passes away and they have to move to the new earth? If they have counted on heaven to be their eternal home, I am afraid they will be disappointed. Both heaven and earth will pass away at some point. Cling to God, who will never pass away. Focus on Him. Let Him be the center of your universe. He is everything you could ever need or want. Patient waiting before Him will teach all of us these all-important lessons.

How Long Do We Have to Wait?

Although the psalmist declared, *"I waited patiently for the Lord; and he inclined unto me, and heard my cry"* (Psalm 40:1), we often wonder why it seems to take God so long to hear us. Actually, He hears us the very first time we cry, but He does not always respond immediately. This may be for a variety of reasons. One of them could be that we are not approaching God with the right attitude, and He has to allow us to "stew" for a while so that we can see the error of our ways. If He is not satisfied with the condition of our hearts, He may delay His answer.

This reminds me of the way Peruvian potters perfect their vessels. In that country, there is an area of very excellent soil for pottery, and that soil has attracted some of the best potters to the place. There they still fire their vessels in a crude open oven, and one can observe the pottery as it bakes.

Those who have vessels in the oven go about their other activities, but they keep an ear tuned to the oven because when a vessel is baked to perfection, it begins to give off a high-pitched tone that lets the potter know that it is time to remove it. When I learned this, I realized that this is exactly what God does with us. He puts us in His oven, and then He listens as He goes about His other work. Always His ear is attuned to us, and when He hears the sounds He desires, He knows that it is time to remove us from the fire.

Don't worry about this process. He is the Master Potter, and He never makes a mistake. You will surely think you should be let out of the oven much sooner, but He always knows best. Wait for His timing. Eventually He will call, "He's done," or "She's done," and the fire will be turned off.

It is difficult to imagine it, but Noah was in the ark with all those animals for more than a year. How would you have liked to be in that floating barn? And there were only eight people to care for so many animals. When the Bible said, *"And God remembered Noah"* (Genesis 8:1), those four little words had great meaning. God's timer went off, and He said, "Okay, Noah's done. Take him out." And the waters subsided enough that the door of the ark could be opened.

Let God work on you until He is finished. In the meantime, allow Him to give you songs in the night—songs in the pit, songs in the fiery furnace, and songs in the lions' den. As David wrote, *"He hath put a new song in my mouth, even praise unto our God: many shall see it, and fear, and shall trust in the LORD"* (Psalm 40:3).

The words of this new song are not something you just dream up. God Himself puts them into your heart and into your mouth, and He does it while you are in your fiery furnace or whatever your current trial happens to be. The result is a reverence, a fear or a trust, in the Lord.

And there is more. Now that you have learned your lesson and are singing to God a new song in the midst of your tribulation, God lifts you out of it, sets your feet upon a rock, and establishes your goings (see Psalm 40:2). He has heard your cry, seen your heart's condition, and brought deliverance. Now your victory is complete.

Oh, my friend, patient waiting is good for the soul.

Patient Waiting Is Good for the Soul

Jesus said:

In your patience [patient waiting] *possess ye your souls.*
Luke 21:19

The meaning from the original Greek text is a better translation. It is *"by your patient waiting provide for your soul."* Why is this true? Patient waiting feeds the soul, and Jesus knew it because He spent years practicing it. He urged His disciples to continue His practice.

Other New Testament writers agree with the need for patient waiting:

For ye have need of patience [patient waiting], *that, after ye have done the will of God, ye might receive the promise.*
Hebrews 10:36

But let patience [patient waiting] *have her perfect work, that ye may be perfect and entire, wanting nothing.*
James 1:4

There is no possible way you can mature without first learning patient waiting. Neither receiving revelation nor possessing spiritual gifts will ever bring you the maturity that patient waiting provides. Run with it.

Run With Patient Waiting

Wherefore seeing we also are compassed about with so great a cloud of witnesses, let us lay aside every weight, and the sin which doth so easily beset us, and let us run with patience [patient waiting] *the race that is set before us.*

Hebrews 12:1

There is no other proper way to run, but to wait, and you can actually wait while you run. If God says to run and you don't, you cannot wait properly, and if He says to wait and you run, you cannot run properly.

At one point in my Christian experience, I was in darkness for two full years, wondering why the Lord seemingly had forsaken me. The reading of the Bible and prayer were not as meaningful to me, and I could not seem to get blessed in church services.

"Why? Why? Why?" my soul kept crying out. It was only after I had finished "whying" God that He was able to deal with me and do the work He needed to do. That did not take Him long at all, and I was soon back on the road of blessing.

At the end of that two-year period, I took a very hard look at what had happened to me and discovered that God had built in me a trust that I could not find words to explain to others. The extent of it was simply inexplicable. That trust kept me through the many life-and-death situations I would face in the years to come while I was in the Amazon and in other countries. I was able to face them calmly, knowing that God had everything under control and that there was no reason for me to get excited or to be worried.

For instance, several interesting things happened while I was on a missionary trip to Costa Rica. Another missionary and myself, along with a national preacher named Marcus, left San Jose, the capital city, by bus and traveled most of the day to a frontier town, where we then took a small plane bound for a remote jungle village.

The Cessna 180 was designed to hold four people and very limited luggage, but the pilot didn't seem to understand that fact. He crammed the luggage compartment until it began to intrude upon the passenger space. In the back seat, built for two, he put us three

135

big men. A woman sat in the front with him. So there were five passengers, three of them large men, and way too much luggage.

To top it all off, the runway sat in a bowl-like valley, with mountains on all sides of it, and I had to wonder how safe it was to try to get that plane into the air with such a heavy load. If the pilot was worried, he didn't show it.

The Cessna rolled down the strip, straining with all it was worth, but then, as I had imagined, it seemed that the pilot could not get it off the ground. As we raced toward the mountain, the pilot broke out in a cold sweat.

Under my breath, I prayed, "God, if this plane doesn't go up, You don't go up either." What I meant by that was that He was with me, so I could relax. If He was faithful (and He had never failed me yet), He would get that plane into the air—somehow.

Sure enough, without even a foot to spare, the plane became airborne, then banked around sharply to avoid the mountain. We were safe—for the moment at least.

It had been raining at the crude village airstrip when we arrived, and it was obvious that the runway was very muddy. Nevertheless, the pilot decided to attempt a landing.

Instead of moving straight ahead after the tires had hit the runway, the plane drifted to the left, and we soon found ourselves moving down the muddy runway sideways.

Why we didn't flip over I will never know, but the pilot was powerless to gain control of the aircraft or to apply the brakes to slow its forward motion. It soon became apparent that we needed a miracle, for the runway ended at the edge of a two-hundred foot cliff. That miracle came. We stopped somehow—just in time and with only a small piece of real estate between us and eternity. Missionary life was proving to be very interesting.

We spent the night in one of the local believers' homes, sleeping in hammocks that we strung up wherever we could. We would need the rest because still ahead of us, the next day, lay the third leg of our journey—a nine-hour hike deep into the jungle hills.

We started early the next morning and had a pleasant walk until we came to a river. The only way to cross, we were told, was to wade it. Large boulders were scattered about its surface, and the current appeared to be devastatingly swift. One thing was sure. We could never swim across that river. The trick would be to locate the spot where we judged the water to be the most shallow. If we got in too deep (chest high), the strong current would carry us unmercifully downstream.

Marcus went first carrying his pack, and he made it across without incident. Next, the other missionary attempted the crossing. In the middle of the river, he was swept off his feet and disappeared under the water. I frantically ran downstream trying to locate him. I wondered if I would ever see him again, but eventually he bobbed up, still clinging to his bag. As he was swept along, he was violently thrown into one boulder after another. Finally, his feet found a gravel bar, and he struggled out of the water onto the opposite bank of the river. He was obviously cut and badly bruised. And now it was my turn to try to cross.

I decided to look for a safer crossing place. A little ways upstream, I seemed to find what I was looking for. The current there seemed much quieter, and I started out with my pack on my back, doing just fine.

Then, just a short distance into the steam, the water suddenly became much deeper, and I found it difficult to resist its pull on me. I froze in place in an attempt to recover my strength and move on, but the current began to wash the gravel out from under my feet where I stood. Suddenly I realized that I was in a dilemma. If I turned now and tried to go back toward the shore, I felt that I would lose my footing entirely and be swept downstream. But I also couldn't go forward. Then, even attempting to keep my footing where I was began draining my strength. Soon, regardless of what I did, I would be carried away by the current.

Becoming the Expression of the Father

Marcus, seeing my plight, prepared to come to my aid. Then suddenly there appeared on the opposite shore, a little upstream from us, a pure white horse with a rider. A pure white colt followed close behind them. Thinking back later, I could not imagine where they had come from because there was no trail coming out of the jungle in that direction.

The rider did not pause or ask any questions but rode quickly into the river and straight for me, reaching me before Marcus could even get into the water. Without a word, the man took the pack from my back and took it to the other side. That gave me the freedom to turn and get back to the other shore. From there, I was able to choose a better spot and make a successful crossing.

As soon as I was safely on the other side, the rider continued his way downstream. He never said a word to any of us. As I thought back on the experience, I realized that I had barely looked at him. The white horse and colt had been so stunningly beautiful that I had given the rider little notice. Never, before or since, had I seen such a horse.

Many thought that the rider must have been the Lord coming to my rescue and intervening to save my life. If so, it wasn't the first time, and it would not be the last.

If I had only realized years before what lay ahead of me, I could have saved myself many "whys". We sometimes "why" God for years on end, even though it does not get us anywhere. Stop "whying" and save yourself some time.

Through these and many other unusual experiences, I came to fully understand the periods of preparation through which the Lord had taken me, and I was grateful. It was the trust we learned in those hard times and dark places, those fiery furnaces of life, that enabled us to commit our children to the Lord in the areas troubled with malaria and not to ever be concerned about the possibility that they would contract it. The trust that we develop in times of patient waiting upon the Lord does not allow us to have such concerns. We are so tightly gripped by it that there is no room for worry and doubt to operate in our spirits.

Such a trust cannot be gained through the acquisition of knowledge. It is a gift from God, rubbed into you over time. And in time, it brings forth fruit:

> *But that on the good ground are they, which in an honest and good heart, having heard the word, keep it, and bring forth fruit with patience* [by patiently waiting].
>
> Luke 8:15

Farmers know this principle. First they prepare their ground. Then they plant, fertilize, and water it. After that it takes patient waiting to receive a crop. Make sure your feet are in proper soil, and patient waiting will indeed produce a harvest in due time.

Many Blessings Are Declared for Those Who Learn Patient Waiting

> *For evildoers shall be cut off: but those that wait upon the Lord, they shall inherit the earth. For yet a little while, and the wicked shall not be; yea, thou shalt diligently consider his place, and it shall not be. But the meek shall inherit the earth; and shall delight themselves in the abundance of peace.*
>
> Psalm 37:9-11

> *But they that wait upon the Lord shall renew their strength; they shall mount up with wings as eagles; they shall run, and not be weary; and they shall walk, and not faint.*
>
> Isaiah 40:31

> *And let us not be weary in well doing: for in due season we shall reap, if we faint not.*
>
> Galatians 6:9

Wait on the LORD: be of good courage, and he shall strengthen thine heart: wait, I say, on the LORD.

Psalm 27:14

The LORD is good unto them that wait for him, to the soul that seeketh him. It is good that a man should both hope and quietly wait for the salvation of the LORD.

Lamentations 3:25-26

Behold, we count them happy which endure. Ye have heard of the patience [patient waiting] *of Job, and have seen the end of the Lord; that the Lord is very pitiful, and of tender mercy.*

James 5:11

Some Closing Thoughts

Some use the idea of waiting as a way of delaying their obedience to God or of disobeying Him entirely. He speaks to them to do something, and they say they will pray about it and wait on the Lord. But, in this case, what is there to pray about? What are they waiting for? Waiting is no substitute for obedience. Those who learn patient waiting upon God are also completely obedient. Waiting is never just an excuse for inaction. Waiting when you already know what to do is unproductive and disobedient.

Would it surprise you to know that the Lord is waiting for you?

And therefore will the LORD wait, that he may be gracious unto you, and therefore will he be exalted, that he may have mercy upon you: for the LORD is a God of judgment: blessed are all they that wait for him.

Isaiah 30:18

How wonderful! The Lord is just waiting to bless you, and He is waiting for you to wait before Him so that you can be blessed. He wants to be gracious unto you and have mercy upon you. And He promises that you will be blessed in your waiting.

So what are you waiting for? Get busy waiting.

If you are among those who find waiting to be the most difficult thing they could be asked to do, don't despair. Just as we can ask the Lord to help us with our agape, we can ask Him to help us in this regard as well:

And the Lord direct your hearts into the love of God, and into the patient waiting for Christ.

2 Thessalonians 3:5

Those who take this stand move to the front of the line to become the expression of the Father in the earth.

Becoming the Expression of the Father

Chapter Ten

LIVING IN THE
RIGHTEOUSNESS OF GOD

*But seek ye first the kingdom of God, and his righteousness; and
all these things shall be added unto you.*

Matthew 6:33

Too often we concentrate on the broad picture of the kingdom of
God and fail to focus on what is so extremely important: developing godly character, His righteousness in us. Another of our
excesses that Jesus addressed here is our obsession with things. We
have already touched on this subject in other contexts, but it is so
important that we must elaborate a little more on it here and relate
it to our true goal—God's righteousness in us, not our own.

Earlier in this chapter of Matthew, Jesus said:

*Lay not up for yourself treasures upon earth, where moth and rust
doth corrupt, and where thieves break through and steal: but lay
up for yourselves treasures in heaven, where neither moth nor rust
doth corrupt, and where thieves do not break through nor steal:
for where your treasure is, there will your heart be also.*

Matthew 6:19-21

Becoming the Expression of the Father

As we have seen, we simply cannot afford to place our attention on earthly things, for they have no lasting value. Even in this life, values change. In one place, something that is considered to be of little value may be treasured elsewhere. Things that were once considered junk to be discarded are suddenly valuable, and people who can afford it pay a premium for them.

Things that we consider to be extremely valuable can also suddenly become worthless. Moths can quickly render a $3,000 coat worthless, and rust can quickly destroy a $50,000 car. And, worse, expensive items can and often do disappear, stolen by someone wanting to take advantage of their worth.

Men go to great lengths to acquire nice things, only to die and not be able to enjoy them or to have them stolen or damaged. In fact, worry about loss or damage afflicts many who own nice things. Jesus gave us the secret of proper living when He said that we should, instead, lay up for ourselves riches in heaven. Spiritual treasures cannot be stolen or damaged. Every Christian needs to take this message very seriously.

The Dangers of Loving Things

Most Christians love "things" just as much as non-Christians do and make the mistake of concentrating on the earthly rather than the eternal. If all of us had put forth as much effort toward obtaining the eternal as we have the earthly, we would be much further along in our spiritual progress.

Somehow we still have not come to value eternal things as the treasures they really are and to deem them profitable and pleasurable enough to go after. In reality, the spiritual realm is above and beyond the earthly in every sense.

Jesus wants to bring us into proper spiritual focus, so He said, *"Where your treasure is, there will your heart be also."* That is the problem. When we are obsessed with accumulating what we consider to be treasures, that is where our hearts will be concentrated. For instance, some have their hearts concentrated on the stock markets. Then, when the bottom suddenly drops out, as has happened in the past and will surely happen again in the future, their hearts go with it. In 1929, when the stock market suffered its most serious crash to date, many people committed suicide. All that they had trusted in disappeared in a moment's time, and they were emotionally devastated by it. To them, all was lost, and life was no longer worth living.

What a tragedy! Why would men place their hopes in something so changeable? When the things we trust fail, then what?

The spiritual realm is above and beyond the earthly in every sense.

A young man I knew well was zealous for God and wanted to serve Him, but he somehow got too focused on earthly things and, for a time, concentrated on accumulating wealth. He may have had a very good motive in this, but in the process his heart became too engrossed with earth's treasures. In the end, he was left bankrupt, both physically and spiritually. He may well have been what James called *"a double minded man"*:

A double minded man is unstable in all his ways.

James 1:8

James warned:

For let not that man think that he shall receive any thing of the Lord.

James 1:7

Trying to go two ways at one time always leads to disaster. Focus on the eternal, and you will win in every sense of the word.

If you are determined to be rich, then go for it, but enjoy it while you can, for it will not last long. If you are determined to be blessed, follow righteousness. But you cannot follow the two paths at once. It won't work. You will end up losing in both areas.

Singleness of Eye

As we have seen, Jesus admonished us to singleness of eye, or in other words, to clear spiritual focus:

The light of the body is the eye: if therefore thine eye be single, thy whole body shall be full of light.

Matthew 6:22

"Single" here denotes concentration on a particular pathway, and such a concentration produces blessing. If a young man decides to become a surgeon, he must give it his all. He cannot study to be a CPA and/or a lawyer at the same time. Each of these professions demands a concentration on the issues relevant to it. Those who divide their attention will not do well at any one thing. When the eye is single, we are enlightened, and each point builds on the last toward a worthy climax.

This term *"full of light"* means "radiant." Have you ever seen a radiant Christian? They are powerful, aren't they?

The strange thing is that those who are radiant and those who are not are all looking to the same God. They are all saved. The difference is in their focus.

Why are some radiant and others are not? There must be a good reason. It all depends on the principles that guide our lives and the pathway we choose to follow. It is the same eye, but the focus is quite different.

If our eyes are focused on darkness, or unrighteousness, then what can we expect to be the outcome? Don't be surprised when the whole being is darkened. This explains why many Christians wallow in melancholy and emotional upset. They never see God and

His righteousness because they are so focused on themselves, their problems, and their negative circumstances.

This also explains why some Christians seem to have learned nothing. They only add darkness to darkness, and as Jesus said, *"How great is that darkness!"* (See Matthew 6:23.)

Some Christians receive counseling, get prayed for, and go through deliverance, yet still continue to sink into darkness. There is a reason. They are like a person who wants to dry himself off, but who continues to stand under a running shower. We want to shout at that person, "Get out from under there, or you will never be able to get dry."

It Is Impossible to Serve Two Masters

No man can serve two masters: for either he will hate the one, and love the other; or else he will hold to the one, and despise the other. Ye cannot serve God and mammon.

Matthew 6:24

We can lay up treasures in either heaven or on earth—not both. We can serve either God or man—not both. Trying to do both will tear you apart. If you love the one, you will hate the other. Choose whom you will serve. You cannot serve both, and we are called to serve only one Master.

In the next verse of His Sermon on the Mount, Jesus came to His *"therefore."* When this word is present in the Bible, we can know that there is a strong connection between what has been said and what is about to be said:

Therefore I say unto you, Take no thought for your life....

Matthew 6:25

This phrase *"take no thought"* teaches us not to divide our attention, not to tear ourselves apart with dual purposes or goals. We cannot be totally concentrated on what we need for everyday living

147

and, at the same time, trying to please God with our lives. The full thought in this verse is this:

Take no thought for your life, what ye shall eat, or what ye shall drink; nor yet for your body, what ye shall put on. Is not the life more than meat, and the body than raiment?

Matthew 6:25

Life is about more than satisfying our fleshly appetites. True life is to be found in God's righteousness. We need food and clothes for our bodies, yes, but we have greater needs that must also be met. If we concentrate on immediate needs, we lose everything, but if we concentrate on the eternal, we gain everything.

Paul wrote to the church at Rome:

Neither yield ye your members as instruments of unrighteousness unto sin: but yield yourselves unto God, as those that are alive from the dead, and your members as instruments of righteousness unto God.

Romans 6:13

This takes a conscious commitment, a decision on our part, one that many are unable to make. I took a Bible school student with me once to a home Bible study I was conducting in a very nice area of town. I thought nothing of being there, but, as it turned out, the student was seriously affected by it. I knew that Cadillacs and Lincolns eventually rust out and break down just like other vehicles do, and they all end up in the same junkyard. I knew that life was not in houses or lands or furniture, but for him, the wealth he saw others enjoying was a problem.

Settle the Issue Once and for All

I had settled this issue long ago. When I was still a third-year Bible school student, I was standing at my window one day in the early afternoon looking out at the girls' dormitory. We were very restricted in our contacts with the girls, and I was hoping to get a glimpse of my girlfriend Violet (who later became my wife) as she was coming out of the dorm.

Suddenly, I saw a first-year student approaching in a brand-new red and white Plymouth (which, I later learned, he had just taken delivery of from the dealer). The car was so beautiful that it looked to me in that moment like a new coin fresh from the mint. It literally gleamed.

My eyes grew as big as saucers as the student proceeded to park his new car directly in front of the girls' dorm where I had been looking. For the moment I forgot all about Violet. The car was all that I could think about.

I was alone in my room, and I said to God, "God, do You see that?" I paused to give Him a few moments to look the shiny new car over.

"Now," I said, "I want You to look over into the parking lot at *my* car. You can't miss it. It's the one with two fenders missing, and it's the only one like that." Again I gave God some time to look over what I was showing Him.

Eventually, I said to God, "Now, I ask You: Is that fair?"

In His kindness and longsuffering, God overlooked my stupidity and my arrogance that day, and He actually answered me. When He did, His answer rang in me like a bell.

"But you have something he doesn't have," He said.

I knew what He meant (He was referring to my spiritual capacity), and when He said it, tears suddenly clouded my vision, and that red and white Plymouth became a blur. From that day to this, fine automobiles have never been my focus. Even if a vehicle is worth a vast sum of money, it is not worth my love and devotion. If I focus on God's righteousness, *"all these things"* (all the things I need for daily living) will be added to me. God has my best interests at heart, so I will trust His will for my life.

This is not to say that we are to go mindlessly through life. God has not called us to act irresponsibly. He has called us to focus on Him and His will.

Trusting God does not mean that we do not work. Lazy people sometimes use that excuse, but Paul was very harsh with lazy people in his writings. He was a very hard worker himself, even though he had suffered a lot for the Lord. Take a moment now and think about. What is your focus in life?

What Is Your Focus?

When we live our lives focused on things, we are no better than unbelievers, as Jesus showed:

> *(For after all these things do the Gentiles seek:) for your heavenly Father knoweth that ye have need of all these things.*
>
> Matthew 6:32

How about you? Is your focus any different from that of the unbelievers around you?

God is not uninterested in our daily needs, and He expects us to bring them before Him in prayer. What is sad to me, though, is that many Christians never get beyond that point. They never discover the loving provision of the Father that allows us to rest in Him daily and not worry about anything. In reality, God wants to give us more than we can even think or ask. He wants to shower His love upon us like the bride we are:

> *I am my beloved's, and his desire is toward me.*
>
> Song of Solomon 7:10

What a discovery this is! Nothing compares with coming to know and experience the richness and vastness of the provisions in the desire of God toward us. As we lay aside our own desires (I personally do not

150

trust my own desires at all), we begin to receive what He desires for us, and that is always better.

We must lay aside our desires to receive what the Father desires.

Many Christians cannot handle this truth because it would absolutely destroy their prayer life, which is based entirely on their perceived needs. Only when we are loosed from these personal desires can we carry the yoke the Father places upon us, allowing us to bear a burden for others.

Seek His righteousness, and you will be surprised. All the other things you need will come to you.

Why Do Men Go About Developing Their Own Righteousness?

For they being ignorant of God's righteousness, and going about to establish their own righteousness, have not submitted themselves unto the righteousness of God.

Romans 10:3

This letter was not written to the heathen, and it does not speak of the heathen. In verse 2, the people in question are described as having *"a zeal for God."* Still, their failure was an unwillingness to submit themselves to the righteousness of God. Could it be that the righteousness of God demanded too much of them? And what exactly is "the righteousness of God"?

The righteousness of God is not, as many have believed, a list of rules. It is a way of life based on our relationship to God and His workings in us. Those who are unwilling to live a life that is pleasing to Him go about to establish their own codes of ethics and conduct. To them, the Gospel of grace and truth is much too limiting, too restrictive, and too narrow. It does not leave them enough personal liberties.

It is true that when Christ is living in our hearts, we cannot live just any old way we want to live. God's righteousness is one of dignity and respect—respect for Him and respect for one another. It demands that we not mistreat and defraud one another. It forbids husbands and wives to mistreat one another. It calls on children to respect their parents in all things. Those who are unwilling to submit to God's ideas of justice must go about creating one of their own, and our world is clearly void of righteousness.

This will change. One day we will have a new earth, and it will be filled with righteous living:

> *Nevertheless we, according to his promise, look for new heavens and a new earth, wherein dwelleth righteousness.*
>
> 2 Peter 3:13

But until that day, God calls on us to yield to His righteousness and allow Him to work in us to bring forth what is right in the earth.

Sadly, righteousness does not prevail even among those who call themselves Christians. There is, for instance, as much divorce among Christians as there is among other sectors of society. There are as many problems with the children of Christian homes as there are with other homes. And we must ask ourselves why this is true.

The answer has to be that our focus has not been sufficiently on the righteousness of God, but on other things.

I have little sympathy for those who insist on doing their own thing and later wonder why God isn't blessing them. What do they expect? When we are unwilling to go God's way, how can we expect Him to bail us out when we have gotten ourselves into trouble?

The Righteousness of God Produces the Oil of Gladness

Thou hast loved righteousness, and hated iniquity; therefore God, even thy God, hath anointed thee with the oil of gladness above thy fellows.

Hebrews 1:9

Some Christians are so obviously happy. They have personal contentment, a sense of well-being, and fullness in God, and we often wonder why. Well, ponder no more. These people have loved righteousness and hated iniquity, and so God has anointed them with the oil of gladness above their fellows.

When we have God's joy that comes through righteous living, we can wake up every single morning and say, "Isn't it great to be alive." It will not matter what the day looks like, how many pains they are experiencing, or how well their financial plans are progressing. A person who is dying with cancer can still wake up and say, "It's great to be alive."

This is the abundant life, and it is not to be found in the material. Jesus came to give life, and many have that. But He also came to give life abundantly, and far fewer have received that.

Jesus said of those who hunger and thirst for righteousness:

Blessed are they which do hunger and thirst after righteousness: for they shall be filled.

Matthew 5:6

Therefore, make this (God's righteousness in you) the focus of your prayer—not food, clothes, rent money, cars, or anything else.

When Jesus said, *"They shall be filled,"* He did not say what they would be filled with. He left a blank to be filled in by you. It is anything you want, anything you need. It is *"all these things."* It is God's bountiful provision for your life.

Paul prayed a prayer for all of us. It goes like this:

153

Becoming the Expression of the Father

...that ye might be filled with all the fulness of God.
Ephesians 3:19

If that prayer is ever to be answered in your life, things must cease to be the focus of your daily existence, and righteousness must become your goal. Those who take this stance are already in line to become the expression of the Father in the earth.

Chapter Eleven

CLAIMING SUFFICIENCY IN CHRIST

Not that I speak in respect of want: for I have learned, in whatsoever state I am, therewith to be content. I know both how to be abased, and I know how to abound: every where and in all things I am instructed both to be full and to be hungry, both to abound and to suffer need.

Philippians 4:11-12

In this passage, Paul made a very amazing claim. He said that he had self-sufficiency in Christ. This seems like a contradiction, but there is a wonderful truth here that is key to successful Christian living.

My own translation of the Greek of verse 11 would render it, *"I have learned to be self-sufficient in whatever circumstances I am."* The word translated as "content" in the King James Bible is actually composed of two Greek words: *autos* (which we understand as "self") and *archao* (meaning "sufficient, having enough, having a sufficiency"). But when Paul used this term, clearly meaning "self-sufficient," he did

155

not use it in the way we normally understand "self-sufficiency" in English.

In our common usage of this phrase, it means that we are the *source* of the sufficiency, and Paul meant something very different. In his thinking, the believer is not the *source* of the sufficiency, but rather the *location* of the sufficiency. The sufficiency comes from God, but it resides in the believer. This enables the believer to stand firm without outside help.

God, in this sense, is not outside help. He is building for Himself a habitation, and that habitation is you. He has not finished you yet, but He is in the process of making you into what He wants you to be. As He goes about this, He pours into you of Himself—His goodness, His character, His wherewithal—and if you can just surrender to Him and allow Him to complete His work, the end result will be glorious.

Why is it that so very many Christians are suffering from depression, from defeat, and from despondency? In God there is no defeat, only victory. Could it be that we are experiencing so much defeat because we are struggling against what God is trying to do within us? Could we be resisting the manifestation of His life in us?

God is gracious and generous, and He is able to pour His character into us and make us gracious and generous as well. As His character fills us more and more, we become more like Him. He is able to pour into us His sufficiency so that we become victors in every sense of the word.

This particular word meaning "self-sufficient" was used in the Bible only by Paul, and even then he used it only three times. Each time it has the same meaning. God pours into us, building us up and adding to us, so that we become the habitation that He so desires us to become. As He builds us, He tests us, so that we may be firmly established. He does not want to wake up one day to a house that has suddenly caved in.

Angels are never required to be tested as men are. We must be proven and improved upon until no storm can even rattle our windows.

But to get to that place, there is a learning process that we must all go through, and many of us don't like that idea.

The Learning Process

As a boy, I was one of those students who did not like learning. I went to school for fun, not to learn. My teachers tried to help me learn, but I had the idea that it was just a matter of passing through the grades successfully so that I could be finished with the entire process and get on with real life. Anyway, I thought I already knew everything I needed to know. I wonder now how that could have been possible because it seems the more I learn, the more I need to learn, and the older I get the more ignorant I seem to be (because I realize that there is so much more to be learned).

I am learning, and we must never stop learning. There is no such thing as having "arrived" in God. There will always be new challenges for the believer. You will not bump your head on the ceiling one day and suddenly realize that there is no more growing to be done. And neither can anything limit you in God but yourself. There is a wealth of knowing in Him, and you will never even scratch the surface—even if you are always learning.

Paul had learned many important things in life, and now he knew: *"I know both how to be abased, and I know how to abound: every where and in all things I am instructed both to be full and to be hungry, both to abound and to suffer need"* (Philippians 4:12). This *"I know"* was experiential. It had nothing to do with the knowing that comes by reading or by listening to others. Paul knew by experience how to be abased (that is, to live at the bottom of the barrel), and he knew by experience how to abound (that is, to live at the top). He had been instructed, or disciplined, to know how to react in fullness and in hunger, in abundance and in deficiency.

The Need for Discipline

This word *abased* means being lowered, or coming to a place of suffering. That sounds like a place of discipline to me. In building you to function as He wants you to function, God must develop discipline in you.

We are all self-indulgent to one degree or another, and often God cannot get us to the place He desires because we literally refuse to be disciplined. He must first attempt to work discipline into our hearts and lives, and one of the ways He does that is to deprive us of money for a time. When we cannot buy what we are accustomed to buying, we bow to Him.

Some never learn discipline, and they also never recover financially. Others learn discipline, and they are restored. If you can take something positive away from the unpleasant experience of being deprived for a time, it will signify great gain for you.

Oddly enough, experiencing fullness also can be a place of discipline, and, believe it or not, it is harder to do well while having plenty than it is to do well while suffering want. Poverty disciplines us much faster than plenty does.

I know what I'm saying, for I was tested on it. Once, for instance, someone sent me a check for $5,000, and, at the time, that was *a lot* of money for me. The check was made out to me, and no specific purpose was indicated, so it seemed that I could do with it what I wanted. For a moment my mind ran wild, and I imagined many ways that I could spend the money. Then I came down to earth again and remembered how God had accustomed me to believe Him for my needs. Everything He gave me was for a specific purpose, and so this must be too.

In fact, I had never had this quantity of money in my hand at one time before, so I was not sure just how to react. One thing was certain: I did not want to mishandle the money and have to be sorry later and to pay for such a mistake.

I decided to just put the check away for a few days and wait to see what would happen. Within a week, two serious emergencies arose for which I needed that money (except for my tithes on it), and I was then back to trusting God for my needs from day to day.

If I had spent the money on other things, those emergency needs would not have been met.

When we do well, we must discipline ourselves to be wise stewards of what we have so that God can trust us with more. Too often we act foolishly with what He places in our hands. In this way, His supply is a test of our resolve for the kingdom.

Experiencing All Grace

The second use of this term, meaning self-sufficiency, is found in Paul's second letter to the Corinthians:

> *And God is able to make all grace abound toward you; that ye, always having all sufficiency in all things, may abound to every good work.*
>
> 2 Corinthians 9:8

The original Greek of this verse says: *"God is able to make abound toward you all grace* [that is a lot of grace] *and in all circumstances* [that covers a lot of territory], *that always* [that covers a lot of time] *having total self-sufficiency* [that fills up the cup], *you may abound in every good work* [you may be abundant in everything]."

To my way of thinking, this is one of the greatest promises in the entire Bible. If every believer could just move his or her life into the truth of that verse, or have the truth of that verse move into his or her life, just think what he or she could become.

How amazing! God has for you all grace (all the grace you will ever need), in all circumstances. So it does not really matter how the wind is blowing, and neither does it matter what is happening around you. As you pass through the many storms in this life, you can know that God is still on the throne. He will see you through every storm because He has all grace for you—no matter what circumstances you are facing at the moment. His promise is that you will always have total self-sufficiency, not just six months out of the year, but *always*.

As He pours into you, His grace does not wear thin and His strength does not run out. His strength and His grace are unending, and He can pour and pour into you and still have plenty left over where that came from.

God's grace does not wear thin and His strength does not run out.

This passage only confirms the fact that the circumstances of life should never sway us or shape or guide our lives. Circumstances—whether they are for or against you—are just that—circumstances. Battle through them and get victory over them. Sometimes it seems that all hell has broken loose against you, but so what? You can overcome any circumstance.

We are in God, and He is on the throne. Circumstances are not ruling the universe, and neither are the forces of hell. Many Christians are terrified by evil spirits, but you should never be worried about them. Every one of them must bow to our Lord. Satan, the prince of evil (although he does a good job at what he does), frequently plays into the hands of believers, and what he does actually turns to our good. He does not know it, but he is God's servant, and he is your servant too.

When he tries to kill you, all he does is drive you closer to the Lord and make you more determined and powerful. When he tries to defeat you by weakening you, the only thing he accomplishes is to bring you more victory because he drives you into the arms of Jesus. Everything he does is turned against his own designs. I like that. Our God is still on the throne, and all things are under His control.

Some tremble at the presence of principalities and powers, but not I. I don't care what they happen to be or who they happen to be under. All I know is that they are under God's feet and, because of that, they are under my feet too. God is looking down on it all, and in Him I can look down on it all too. He is supreme, and as His child I share in His supremacy.

Enjoying the Abundant Life

The third use of "self-sufficient" in the New Testament is found in the words Paul wrote to Timothy:

Godliness with contentment [self-sufficiency] *is great gain.*

1 Timothy 6:6

Jesus admonished us not to become unduly concerned about the issues of everyday life. We are to enjoy the abundant life He offers and to remain free in our spirits. We don't depend on this present world system. That is not our source; God is. Like the enemies of the children of Israel, some will trust in chariots, but we don't have to join them. We cannot afford to put our trust in earthly things. Jeremiah declared that the man who did it would be cursed (see Jeremiah 17:5).

That does not mean that we can never trust anyone. The problem comes when we put our trust in people and not in God.

The story is told of a man who needed tires for his car. He had no money to pay for them, so he made sure that he got next to a man who owned the local tire shop as the people prayed around the altar of the church. As they all prayed out loud, he prayed for his tires, hoping the tire man would overhear him and want to help him. This is not exactly what God had in mind for prayer. We are to touch the heart of God, not necessarily the heart of man. God will take care of that part of it.

Becoming the Expression of the Father

Trust in God. Your destiny was contemplated in the Father's heart before Adam was created. You were in the heart of God before any creation began. Unfortunately, with the fall, man lost God's original intention. Isaiah stated:

All we like sheep have gone astray; we have turned every one to his own way; and the LORD hath laid on him the iniquity of us all.

Isaiah 53:6

All of us have strayed from the Father's heart. All of us have turned to our own ways, and now Jesus calls us back to our rightful place.

When we are born into this world, we come emptied of the heart of God. He wants to pour into us of Himself and bring us back to His heart—with abundance.

Dying "Full"

After all is said and done here on earth, we should be able to die *"full."* Let me explain what I mean by that.

Most people work hard in this life to gather all the goods they can, they have their short fling, and then they die. Too often they die empty.

When a wealthy man died, one of his daughters asked the lawyer overseeing his estate what he had left. The answer was, "He left it all." The man had left this world empty.

Abraham lived a long life, but he left with more than most:

And these are the days of the years of Abraham's life which he lived, an hundred threescore and fifteen years. Then Abraham gave up the ghost, and died in a good old age, an old man, and full of years; and was gathered to his people.

Genesis 25:7-8

One hundred and seventy-five years was certainly a ripe old age, but Abraham was blessed with more than long years of life. In the

162

King James Version there are two words in this verse that are italicized, signifying that they were added by the translators. They are the words *"of years."* The original text stated: *"Abraham...died...full."* In other words, he did not die empty, as most men do.

True, Abraham was not able to take any gold or silver with him, and neither could he take any goats, cattle, or servants. But he *"died...full."*

Abraham was known as a righteous man and a friend of God, a distinction that only one other man held (Moses). Abraham died *"full"* because he gathered from God during his lifetime.

You, too, can be an Abraham. God is ready to pour into your life, of His grace and His riches, to fill you up so that when you leave this earth, you will be loaded. You will leave with great spiritual riches.

And, as we have seen, the fullness of what you gather here will then become a platform, or foundation, from which God can launch you into your destiny in eternity. Some will go to heaven with a foundation, or basis, upon which to their future can be built, and some will go without one. If you have faithfully gathered from God, there the Lord will say, *"You have been faithful,"* and this will be the foundation from which He projects you to greater things.

This, then, is an important time, for your foundations are being laid, and the strength of them will determine your hereafter.

Triumphing Over Circumstances

Paul's teachings on overcoming circumstances are important ones that deserve to be explored further. As we saw in Chapter Nine, God places us in uncomfortable situations because He does not want us to be controlled by the circumstances of life. Our response is often just the opposite of what He hopes for. We focus on the conditions, the state of the economy, or whatever, and we get totally swept up in our surroundings. This is not what the Lord is expecting of us. He wants us to be in a situation without being controlled by it.

We are never to take our cues from the circumstances of life— whatever they happen to be at the moment. We are never to be controlled by the ebb and flow of the world's monetary systems, for example. We are never to be bound by the material—whether it be a lack of it or an overabundance of it. The Lord is our God, and we will take our cues from Him and Him only.

We must never bow before circumstances or allow them to turn our eyes from God. We must never be swept away by good circumstances or discouraged by bad circumstances. Rather than wallow at the feet of uncomfortable circumstances, bow your knee to God.

The psalmist declared:

He that dwelleth in the secret place of the most High shall abide under the shadow of the Almighty.

Psalm 91:1

The man who will be blessed is not the one cowering under the shadow of every impending storm of life. We must live under the shadow of the Almighty, not under the impact of each day's events. The Almighty rules and reigns in our lives, and no circumstance— not even what we consider to be a catastrophe—can be allowed to overwhelm us. He is above all circumstances and all so-called catastrophes, and He can lift us up above them all. He can give us the wings of an eagle so that we can fly above the storms of life.

It is not inevitable that we be carried away by the blows life deals to us. It is not inevitable that we be overwhelmed with grief. We are not destined for defeat, but we are to be overcomers, and, indeed, more than overcomers in Christ (see Romans 8:37).

The history of the Bible shows men and woman as they faced the situations of life. Some of them chose to face them with God by their sides, and others chose to face them alone. The outcome was always instructive, and from these personal histories we can learn to live above the storms that assail us.

You do not have to be dragged down and discouraged by people and events. Isaiah foretold:

> *Every valley shall be exalted, and every mountain and hill shall be made low: and the crooked shall be made straight, and the rough places plain.*
>
> Isaiah 40:4

Why was this to happen? It was so that you could walk on level ground. Your walk with God was not intended to mimic the ups and downs of life. You can maintain your spiritual equilibrium through everything life throws at you. In one sense, there will be many mountains and many valleys in your walk with God. But in another very real sense, there will be no mountains and no valleys in your life because of His presence with you.

You may indeed face extremes of circumstances, but God will always be the same. At one moment you may have a million dollars in your hand, and at another moment your house may burn down and you lose everything you have with it. Neither extreme must be allowed to affect your walk with God.

Extreme circumstances do not change the constancy of God.

There are circumstances that God has designed to come your way, but these are never intended to do you harm or to move you out of the Way. They are designed for your training and to allow you to see God at work for you in every type of circumstance.

Paul was often caught up in extremes of circumstances, but he was never defeated by them. For instance, he was caught in a tragic storm at sea as he was on his way to Rome. This particular storm was so terrible that neither sun nor stars were visible for some two weeks straight. Everyone on board had given up hope of surviving it.

Then Paul suddenly spoke to the gathered passengers and crew. He told them not to worry, that no one would die, even though the ship would be lost. How could Paul be so positive in the face of such peril? He said that he had heard from an angel in the night:

> *For there stood by me this night the angel of God, whose I am, and whom I serve, saying, Fear not, Paul; thou must be brought before Caesar: and, lo, God hath given thee all them that sail with thee. Wherefore, sirs, be of good cheer: for I believe God, that it shall be even as it was told me.*
>
> Acts 27:23-25

Like Paul, we must choose to believe God, not the circumstances, the affliction, the problem, the difficulty, or anything running contrary to what God has said. When He speaks, it happens, and that settles it.

Having the Mind of Christ

We don't like being in storms, though, and when we are hurting, we want out. We don't want to hurt anymore, we don't want to be uncomfortable, and we are tired of being inconvenienced. When we think in this way, it is clear that we do not have the mind of Christ. When we live with the mind of Christ (as we are called to do), everything changes. Christ willingly suffered and even died, in the process taking upon Himself the form of a servant. He refused to live a life of personal comfort, refused to cater to His personal feelings, and refused to reject personal lack, personal pain, and personal suffering. Instead, He was determined to live His life for us and was willing to do whatever was necessary to that end.

This example is not impossible to emulate, as many believe. Peter wrote to the early Christians:

For even hereunto were ye called: because Christ also suffered for us, leaving us an example, that ye should follow his steps.

1 Peter 2:21

There is clearly something from the previous verse or verses to which Peter was referring when he said, *"For even hereunto were ye called."* In the previous verse he had said:

For what glory is it, if, when ye be buffeted for your faults, ye shall take it patiently? but if, when ye do well, and suffer for it, ye take it patiently, this is acceptable with God.

1 Peter 2:20

So the way we can follow Christ's example is to be willing to suffer wrong—even when we have done nothing to deserve it. Therefore, when we find ourselves in situations not to our liking, our first prayer should not be to get *out* of them but to learn *from* them what God intended all along.

Jesus was God, and so He could have cried for ten thousand angels to come and take Him down from the cross and defeat His enemies. He had that right, and He had that power. Instead, He chose to suffer for us, and we must choose to suffer for Him. His prayer in the garden revealed His own desire, but also His willingness to do the Father's will.

Father, if thou be willing, remove this cup from me: nevertheless not my will, but thine, be done.

Luke 22:42

Of course Jesus wanted out of that situation. He was fully man as well as fully God. Still, He deferred to the Father, and so should we. Usually we use all our energies on insisting on getting out of our situations, and this puts us at cross-purposes with God.

Why is it that we are always insisting on the easy way out? Doing so shows that we are living for ourselves. Why was Jesus willing to set

His own will aside? It showed that He was living for others. He was willing to be the broken bread and the poured-out wine so that our lives could be enriched.

Self-centeredness causes us to press forward with what we want when we want it and in the way we want it. And, in the process, we lose, for what we want is usually not God's very best for us. It is submission to the Father's will, not insistence on our own, that brings us the best life has to offer.

What Will You Settle For?

Our unwillingness to suffer any inconvenience often causes us to lose God's best. He has destined us for wonderfully productive lives, but we often settle for comfort and ease instead. He has set a high place for us, but we often settle for some lower post that somehow looks better to us. At the very least, it looks easier. If you are willing, God is able to lift you up and to do a work in your heart that will not only make you an overcomer, but also will cause you to one day rule and reign with Him.

Those who thus show themselves willing to learn from the good and the bad get in line to become the expression of the Father in the earth.

Chapter Twelve

INHERITING THE KINGDOM

...they which do such things shall not inherit the kingdom of God.
Galatians 5:21

It is one thing to be saved and quite another thing to inherit the kingdom of God. Once we have been brought into the kingdom, we must then go through a process that moves us toward a state of qualification in character and ability. How far we move along in that process determines whether or not we will actually inherit and to what extent.

Hinds' Feet for High Places

If we are to walk on high places, we need what the Scriptures call *"hinds' feet"*:

Yet I will rejoice in the LORD, I will joy in the God of my salvation. The LORD God is my strength, and he will make my feet like hinds' feet, and he will make me to walk upon mine high places.

Habakkuk 3:18-19

Becoming the Expression of the Father

The *"high places"* spoken of in the Scriptures were very physically challenging and very precarious, with little place to gain a foothold. Only those who have gone through the process and allowed the Lord to make their feet *"like hinds' feet"* can successfully walk in such elevated places.

We are not born with hinds' feet; it is only the work of God in us that can give us such ability. How wonderful that He is willing to make my feet, which are not *"like hinds' feet,"* to become *"like hinds' feet"*! This is cause for rejoicing. This working of God in us brings great pleasure to us, and it is a real source of encouragement.

The great salvation that God brings to us is amazing enough in itself, and every child of God begins at that same starting line. But walking in high places is something else entirely. How can we do that? Those who try it without having their feet re-made *"like hinds' feet"* soon fall.

The high places that God has in mind for you represent your portion, your inheritance, your rightful place. But because you are not born with hinds' feet, as God lifts you higher, you may stumble and wonder how you will continue to climb. He sometimes knocks every prop out from under you on purpose, removing all your crutches. Suddenly you find that you can hardly walk at all, and you wonder what God is doing. But don't worry. He is making your feet *"like hinds' feet."* Soon enough you will learn to walk with Him in the high places.

This does not happen overnight. It is a process, and God will have to "do a job on you" a few times until your character is shaped and established sufficiently to ascend.

The psalmist also spoke of the *"high places"* and our need to have *"hinds' feet"* to walk there:

He maketh my feet like hinds' feet, and setteth me upon my high places.

Psalm 18:33

Are you set upon your high places yet? You must be before you can rightfully inherit the kingdom.

Inheriting Demands Maturity

Inheriting demands maturity. Paul wrote to the Galatian church:

Now I say, That the heir, as long as he is a child, differeth nothing from a servant, though he be lord of all.

Galatians 4:1

The son in question was a child, so he could not inherit his father's estate. In his childish condition, he could not function as *"lord of all,"* although that was his right. In one sense, he was already *"lord of all,"* but only by position, only in possibility, only in potential, not by actual possession and not in reality.

If a father died, could his three-year-old son who had inherited everything give specific orders to his servants? Could he oversee his father's (and now his) estate? He might try, but the result would surely not be very satisfying.

Inheriting is far more than a legal right; it is the ability to operate within that legal right. Those who inherit must be able to move into their inheritance and function in it, and, if not, their inheritance is only on paper. It is not yet a reality.

A child may have legal authority, but what difference does that make? Authority without the ability to operate in that authority is somehow false. Real inheritance comes when the person inheriting has the capability to make the necessary decisions and take the necessary actions to operate what has been left to him.

Inheriting is far more than a legal right; it is the ability to operate within that legal right.

Becoming the Expression of the Father

You could inherit millions of dollars, but if you did nothing more than carry it around in a backpack and get it out once in a while to play with it, count it, or show it off to others, that money would not significantly change your life. Unless you had enough sense to put such a sum of money to good use (investing it wisely), it would be meaningless beyond being a great toy.

Year after year you could brag that you had millions of dollars, but so what? You would be no better off than anyone else around you for all that you had inherited.

God does not give an inheritance to someone who would just carry it around and boast about it. He wants each of us to function in our inheritance, to manage it, to use it wisely for our own blessing and for the furtherance of His kingdom. It is not enough to step into what is yours. You must fully possess it, and then you must govern it with authority. You must move into and take control of areas that God has reserved for you.

No one is ready to place a three-year-old on the throne. A king may die, but if his heir is immature, a regent will rule in his place. The child may hold a title, but real governance will come only after he is of proper age. As wonderful as the heir may be, if he is not qualified, no one can run the risk of handing real power over to him.

Jesus taught about a master who had a faithful servant, whom he rewarded:

And he said unto him, Well, thou good servant: because thou hast been faithful in a very little, have thou authority over ten cities.
Luke 19:17

What good would it do to have authority over ten cities without the ability to function in that authority?

Paul Had Sacrificed for His Converts

After describing the child inheritor in Galatians 4, Paul went on:

Inheriting the Kingdom

I am afraid of you, lest I have bestowed upon you labour in vain.
Galatians 4:11

He had invested much into the Galatian believers, as he had into all his converts. For their sakes, he had suffered. At one point, he had been stoned so severely that he was left for dead, and his list of other sufferings was a long one. Still, the disciples of Galatia seemed to be spiritually immature. In fact, they were downright childish in that they were still living in bondage to the elements of the world (see Galatians 4:3-7). Had Paul's sacrifice been in vain? Were the Galatians determined to continue living in bondage, thus limiting their ability to inherit?

Later in that same chapter, Paul wrote:

Nevertheless what saith the scripture? Cast out the bondwoman and her son: for the son of the bondwoman shall not be heir with the son of the freewoman.
Galatians 4:30

This was Paul's great concern, that after having been redeemed from bondage to the world, the Galatians would return to it. He said so in no uncertain terms in verse 9:

But now, after that ye have known God, or rather are known of God, how turn ye again to the weak and beggarly elements, whereunto ye desire again to be in bondage?

These brethren may not have returned to drunkenness and murder, and they may have continued going to church and publicly praising the Lord, but slowly they had drifted back into bondage. Theirs was a religious bondage. They were now speculating about who was (and who was not) circumcised among them and who was (and who was not) keeping the Sabbath. They had left fornication and murder, only to fall into the grip of other nasty things. Paul wrote to them very forcefully:

Becoming the Expression of the Father

Behold, I Paul say unto you, that if ye be circumcised, Christ shall profit you nothing.

Galatians 5:2

The Galatians had not fallen back into bondage on their own accord. Some outsiders who were inclined to this type of religious bondage had come to visit them, and the innocent Galatians had listened to these men and followed their advice. These outsiders were like many people today. They believed that it was necessary to wear a certain type of clothing, constantly consult their do and do-not lists, and never smile. That is what being holy meant to them, and the same can be said for many Christians today.

Religious bondage is just as dangerous as any other type of sin. It will surely prevent us from inheriting just as much as drunkenness will. Paul therefore warned the Galatians that they were in danger of losing their reward:

Christ is become of no effect unto you, whosoever of you are justified by the law; ye are fallen from grace.

Galatians 5:4

He also reminded them:

But when the fulness of the time was come, God sent forth his Son, made of a woman, made under the law, to redeem them that were under the law, that we might receive the adoption of sons. And because ye are sons, God hath sent forth the Spirit of his Son into your hearts, crying, Abba, Father. Wherefore thou art no more a servant, but a son; and if a son, then an heir of God through Christ.

Galatians 4:4-7

Because the Galatians had come into a position of sonship, they were in line to inherit. This was their potential as they were brought into the kingdom of God. They could possess the kingdom and inherit all things prepared for them by the Father. But the rest was up to them. They would have to enter in and possess what was rightfully theirs, so that they could rule and reign with Christ.

God did not call us into His kingdom so that He could rock us in the cradle all day long and keep a bottle of baby formula in our mouths. He brought us in so that we could be raised up as kings and priests to rule with Him. But, alas, to many, Christ has *"become of no effect."* And they are thus *"fallen from grace."*

Inheriting Through Overcoming

A little later, in chapter 5 of his letter to the Galatians, Paul got very specific:

> *Now the works of the flesh are manifest, which are these; Adultery, fornication, uncleanness, lasciviousness, idolatry, witchcraft, hatred, variance, emulations, wrath, strife, seditions, heresies, envyings, murders, drunkenness, revellings, and such like: of the which I tell you before, as I have also told you in time past, that they which do such things shall not inherit the kingdom of God.*
>
> Galatians 5:19-21

This passage is powerful and important. It says *"they…shall not inherit the kingdom."* Who *"shall not inherit the kingdom"*? Those who were in bondage to the works of the flesh and in bondage to the elements of the world. Some of them were in religious bondage, and they, too, would *" not inherit the kingdom."*

This same truth was emphasized to the Corinthian believers:

> *Know ye not that the unrighteous shall not inherit the kingdom of God? Be not deceived: neither fornicators, nor idolaters, nor adulterers, nor effeminate, nor abusers of themselves with mankind, nor thieves, nor covetous, nor drunkards, nor revilers, nor extortioners, shall inherit the kingdom of God.*
>
> 1 Corinthians 6:9-10

This passage does not refer to being saved or not being saved. It is about Christians inheriting the kingdom of God.

John the Revelator wrote:

He that overcometh shall inherit all things; and I will be his God, and he shall be my son.

Revelation 21:7

We come into an inheritance of all things through overcoming, not by simply being saved. What does it mean to overcome? It is to gain victory over. The Greek form of the word cannot be translated exactly as it appears. It would be *"he that victories shall inherit all things,"* and our word *victory* is a noun, not a verb. We say "to gain a victory" or "to become victorious."

But how can you gain a victory or become victorious if there is no battle? How can you overcome if there is nothing to overcome? This is the reason for many of the difficult and troublesome situations the Lord allows to come into our lives. He is providing us with opportunities to overcome.

Trouble is simply an opportunity to overcome.

Sin is just one of the things that we must overcome. As we begin to have God's character built within us and we learn to move in conjunction with the will of God, we will begin to hate what God hates and love what He loves. We will then lose our propensity to be moved by every wind of doctrine and to follow the inclinations of the flesh. Instead, we become strong in the faith, good soldiers of Christ Jesus.

Those who are strong deny the flesh, deny self, and, instead, take up the cross and follow Him. They do not allow things to rule over them, but they rule over things. Their flesh does not dictate to them what to do; they dictate to their flesh what to do.

God Entrusts Overcomers With His Riches

God knows that He can trust overcomers with His riches. He said:

He that is slow to anger is better than the mighty; and he that ruleth his spirit than he that taketh a city.

Proverbs 16:32

Being a missionary has been a challenge in many ways, and one of them has been financial. When the Lord raised me up, He required that I live on whatever He supplied. I became dependent upon the goodness of God as He moved upon the hearts of others to supply my needs. This was sometimes very challenging.

For instance, when I took my first pastoral position, it was in a small church in the countryside. There were about thirty-five who would wander in to the meetings (counting the dogs). The place had never had a pastor before (the church had been started as an outreach of another congregation). These country people could not provide a salary for their pastor, so when I accepted the position, I was forced to seek employment at a local sawmill. Before I could begin that job, a cousin, who was living nearby, called to suggest that I help him sell insurance to earn some extra money. I gladly accepted.

I was due to begin my work at the sawmill on a Wednesday, but that Sunday night the Lord spoke to me and told me not to take either of those jobs. I called the sawmill the next day and told them that I would not be coming to work there, and I called my cousin to apologize for not being able to accept his kind offer. As I put down the telephone that day, I was flooded by the glory of God, and I knew that I had made the right decision. Trusting God would not always be easy, but from that day forward, I would work for God alone, and He would supply my needs.

Becoming the Expression of the Father

My income was quite small at the beginning, but occasionally someone would come along and give me a substantial offering (in those days, a hundred dollars was "substantial"), and I loved that. A few people became regular givers, and I grew accustomed to their gifts, even expecting them so much that I had the money half spent before it was even given. When I realized what was happening, that I was beginning to trust people and not God as my source, I asked Him to cut this income off before I became dependent upon it and not upon Him. He graciously did that, and this became a pattern for my life. Whenever I was in danger of trusting in people too much, God would cut off the income I had been receiving from those people, and He thus forced me to trust Him.

I rejoiced in this. It was dangerous for me to learn to lean upon the arm of flesh and not to trust God. That would have been too costly. Some ministers allow themselves to be controlled by givers, and that is unhealthy. I determined never to do that. I preferred losing support entirely than to come under undue influence of those who gave. I am sure that this counted much when it came time for the Lord to decide what He would entrust into my hands.

We must rule our own spirits, overcoming every inclination that is not of God—whatever it happens to be. Adultery is not the only sin we must guard against. There are little things, seemingly innocent things, that sneak in to trick us. When we recognize them, we must cut them off quickly before they have a chance to do us harm. We will inherit only if we are overcomers.

We Are Called to Great Responsibility

We are called to a great responsibility in the kingdom of God—a responsibility that will affect all ages to come. Many seem to be content with the idea of going into retirement in heaven, but God is not operating some retirement program. His chosen ones will serve Him day and night for ages to come:

Inheriting the Kingdom

Therefore are they before the throne of God, and serve him day and night in his temple: and he that sitteth on the throne shall dwell among them.

Revelation 7:15

Whatever you do, don't fail to appreciate the opportunity that is presently before you. Esau despised his birthright and sold it for momentary pleasure. Later, he was sorry about what he had done:

For ye know how that afterward, when he would have inherited the blessing, he was rejected: for he found no place of repentance, though he sought it carefully with tears.

Hebrews 12:17

This verb *"would"* in the King James Version of the Bible was used in a couple of different ways. It could show a desire, a wish, or it could be nothing more than a helping verb. There was no way of distinguishing between the two uses. This problem did not exist in the original Greek text. There it is obvious that Esau woke up one day with a strong desire: He wanted very badly to inherit the blessing.

The problem was that it was too late. Esau had despised his inheritance before, and now—even through he repented with tears—he could not go back. This is an important point. We can repent until there are no more tears and until we are "blue in the face," as the old saying goes, and that will do nothing to gain us our inheritance. It does not come that way. You inherit only by qualifying.

God's kingdom is not some game. This is serious business. Jesus said:

To him that overcometh will I grant to sit with me in my throne, even as I also overcame, and am set down with my Father in his throne.

Revelation 3:21

Becoming the Expression of the Father

The crowns God offers are not mere souvenirs. They must be earned. Peter wrote to the believers:

Finally, be ye all of one mind, having compassion one of another, love as brethren, be pitiful, be courteous: not rendering evil for evil, or railing for railing: but contrariwise blessing; knowing that ye are thereunto called, that ye should inherit a blessing.

1 Peter 3:8-9

Inheriting Is Not Automatic; It Demands Character

In order to inherit, certain character development is necessary. For instance, Jesus said:

Blessed are the meek: for they shall inherit the earth.

Matthew 5:5

You are called to develop godly character, and if you are able to do so, it will ensure an inheritance for you in God's kingdom.

God made great promises to the children of Israel concerning their Promised Land:

I am the LORD, and I will bring you out from under the burdens of the Egyptians, and I will rid you out of their bondage, and I will redeem you with a stretched out arm, and with great judgments: and I will take you to me for a people, and I will be to you a God: and ye shall know that I am the LORD your God, which bringeth you out from under the burdens of the Egyptians. And I will bring you in unto the land, concerning the which I did swear to give it to Abraham, to Isaac, and to Jacob; and I will give it you for an heritage: I am the LORD.

Exodus 6:6-8

After God had so strongly promised them that they would inherit the land, did they? The fact is that the generation that

180

received this promise perished in the wilderness, and those receiving the final promise from Moses (and the fulfillment through Joshua) were the children and grandchildren. God is faithful to His promises, but men often fail, and when they do, God is forced to pass the promise He has made on to others.

God has promised to make your feet like hinds' feet, but it takes more than words to see it come to pass. We must become obedient to God to the extent that He can fulfill His words in us.

The psalmist said of those who failed God in the wilderness, that they had *"limited the Holy One of Israel":*

Yea, they turned back and tempted God, and limited the Holy One of Israel. They remembered not his hand, nor the day when he delivered them from the enemy.

Psalm 78:41-42

Can we limit the limitless One? Yes, we can cut off His arms so that He cannot bring us into our rightful inheritance. He wants to do it, and He has promised to do it, but He cannot do it without our cooperation.

Jesus Wept Over Jerusalem's Failure

Jesus wept over Jerusalem, showing His great desire for that city:

And when he was come near, he beheld the city, and wept over it, saying, If thou hadst known, even thou, at least in this thy day, the things which belong unto thy peace! but now they are hid from thine eyes.

Luke 19:41-42

O Jerusalem, Jerusalem, thou that killest the prophets, and stonest them which are sent unto thee, how often would I have gathered thy children together, even as a hen gathereth her chickens under her wings, and ye would not! Behold, your house is left unto you desolate.

Matthew 23:37-38

The Lord's desire toward Jerusalem should have been apparent to all, but His arms were restrained in blessing her. He could not do it. The writer of Hebrews urged:

Let us therefore fear, lest, a promise being left us of entering into his rest, any of you should seem to come short of it.

Hebrews 4:1

This was not written to unbelievers, but to *"holy brethren"* (see Hebrews 3:1).

There remaineth therefore a rest to the people of God. For he that is entered into his rest, he also hath ceased from his own works, as God did from his. Let us ["holy brethren"] labour therefore to enter into that rest, lest any man fall after the same example of unbelief [that of the Israelites in the wilderness].

Hebrews 4:9-11

They fell because of disobedience, so we cannot return to inheritance simply through repentance. Instead, we must do as Paul urged:

I beseech you therefore, brethren, by the mercies of God, that ye present your bodies a living sacrifice, holy, acceptable unto God, which is your reasonable service.

Romans 12:1

In short, we must rule our spirits and deny fleshly lusts in this life if we are to rule in the life to come. If we are not faithful to that which God has placed in our care now, how can we expect Him to entrust to us something more in the future? Jesus said:

Inheriting the Kingdom

He that is faithful in that which is least is faithful also in much: and he that is unjust in the least is unjust also in much. If therefore ye have not been faithful in the unrighteous mammon, who will commit to your trust the true riches? And if ye have not been faithful in that which is another man's, who shall give you that which is your own?

Luke 16:10-12

Inheriting the kingdom, sitting on the throne of God, ruling and reigning, having great riches placed at your disposal and great responsibility placed in your care all come through proving yourself faithful to God. May each of us determine to avoid idling away the hours committed to us. May each of us avoid the shame that comes with unfaithfulness and slothful living. Rather, let us properly occupy until our Lord comes. Let us awake from sleep, put on our garments of righteousness, and become involved in the spiritual battle of our time.

Stop walking around on cloud nine and get involved in the work of the hour. Stop being conformed to the world and start conforming to the Word. Surrender your personal desires and accept God's will for your life. No longer permit the flashy lure of the world to determine the pathway you take.

Eternity is at stake, and your decision is one of life and death. Fall to the ground and die, and let God bring forth something new and wonderful from your life. What is at stake? It is becoming the expression of the Father here on earth and throughout eternity.

Becoming the Expression of the Father

Chapter Thirteen

EARNING GOD'S TRUST

He that is faithful in that which is least [little or insignificant] *is faithful also in much: and he that is unjust in the least is unjust also in much. If therefore ye have not been faithful in the unrighteous mammon, who will commit to your trust the true riches?*

Luke 16:10-11

Too often we have considered faithfulness to God to be all-important and faithfulness in other matters of little or no importance. It will surely come as a shock to many that God sees as significant what we do in the seemingly unimportant moments of life. He cannot entrust to us spiritual things until He has found us faithful in the small matters that come before us on a daily basis. How we operate when confronted with small things will determine when we are ready for greater things, for nothing is insignificant in the eyes of God. Also, if we are not faithful with things that belong to someone else, God cannot give us things of our own.

Things, for the most part, are neither righteous nor unrighteous. They can be used for both righteousness and unrighteousness. How we use them is up to us. If we use them for good, more will be placed into our hands. Our goal is to receive *"the true riches,"* but that cannot happen until we learn to be faithful in the things that seem to have little spiritual value.

The next verse goes on to say:

And if ye have not been faithful in that which is another man's, who shall give you that which is your own?"

Luke 16:12

If and when we are found faithful in *"the least"* and faithful with what belongs to others, then the Lord can commit to us His riches. He commits those riches to us for safekeeping, yes, but more so for investment.

It Is Yours

There is another great truth here:

*Who shall give you that which is **your own**?*

Luke 16:12

It is already ours. The Lord has kept many treasures in store for us, but they are ours. Notice what the Scriptures clearly say:

*...he will make me to walk upon **mine** high places.*

Habakkuk 3:19

*...hold that fast which thou hast, that no man take **thy** crown.*

Revelation 3:11

Aside from the many treasures that God has laid up for each of us, there are many other things that belong to Him that He longs to entrust to our care. Jesus taught:

For the kingdom of heaven is as a man travelling into a far country, who called his own servants, and delivered unto them his goods.

Matthew 25:14

These servants did not receive their own goods; the goods belonged to their master. Later the master returned, called his servants, and demanded to know how well they had used the assets he had entrusted to them. One man, for instance, had received five talents, and fortunately he had used them well:

> *Then he that had received the five talents went and traded with the same, and made them other five talents.*
>
> Matthew 25:16

The proper use of the goods entrusted to His servants pleases the Lord, for He always expects a harvest, or a return, on His investment. When His seed is sown, He expects to see a harvest. If we take what the Lord has given us and use it to touch others for Him, there is a resultant harvest that brings Him pleasure. He is pleased when you sow into the lives of others, and that produces more of His goods. Thus the Lord's goods are multiplied through your proper use of them.

Invest God's goods into others for a harvest that pleases God.

As we have seen, when you do this, you never lose. You are always blessed in the process:

> *And he that watereth shall be watered also himself.*
>
> Proverbs 11:25

As we water, or give out to others, there is an automatic response from the Lord. He pours back to us, and it happens simultaneously. We pour out, and He pours back into us. Perhaps more importantly, as we give out, we are showing our faithfulness to Him by producing the desired return on His invested assets.

Becoming the Expression of the Father

This is not salvation by good works. In reality, He does the work, not you:

For it is God which worketh in you both to will and to do of his good pleasure.

Philippians 2:13

Production Is Important

Still, producing something for God is important. Your works reveal your character. If you are generous and merciful and if you are grateful to God for what you have, that fact will be shown in your treatment of others.

He longs to say to you:

Well done, thou good and faithful servant: thou hast been faithful over a few things, I will make thee ruler over many things: enter thou into the joy of thy lord.

Matthew 25:21

But He cannot say that until your faithfulness has been proven. That is why Jesus taught the people around Him that one day the Father would say to His faithful ones:

For I was an hungered, and ye gave me meat: I was thirsty, and ye gave me drink: I was a stranger, and ye took me in: naked, and ye clothed me: I was sick, and ye visited me: I was in prison, and ye came unto me.

Matthew 25:35-36

Those who hear this will be surprised and will ask when this happened. They cannot remember it. Then, said, Jesus:

And the King shall answer and say unto them, Verily I say unto you, Inasmuch as ye have done it unto one of the least of these my brethren, ye have done it unto me.

Matthew 25:40

So, helping others is the greatest investment we can make. It represents doing *"the will of* [the] *Father which is in heaven"*:

> *Not every one that saith unto me, Lord, Lord, shall enter into the kingdom of heaven; but he that doeth the will of my Father which is in heaven.*
>
> Matthew 7:21

The Greek word *basileia* translated here as "kingdom" means more than that. It is kingdom plus reign. So those who enter His kingdom and reign with Him will be those who do the Father's will.

Again, there is a difference between simply being saved and entering into the kingdom of heaven. The only qualification for salvation is to believe, but the qualifications to enter into the kingdom are much more advanced.

We are saved by grace, but entering into the kingdom depends largely on the works that we do, on how well we have utilized what the Lord has placed within our hands. So this passage, like others we have examined in this book, does not deal with being saved. It deals with a job that needs to be done, a function, an operation. God wants to entrust into your hands certain operations in His kingdom, but you can receive them only by proving your faithfulness.

The Complexity of the Kingdom

The kingdom of God is extremely complex. In God's kingdom, literally trillions of people must be fit into specific roles and functions, each one having a specific responsibility to fulfill. But to even get that far, you must qualify.

Of course, no one can qualify for the kingdom without being saved, but we should never confuse salvation with the right to enter and rule in the kingdom. They are two different things.

━━◆━━

Salvation provides entrance into the kingdom; faithfulness determines service in the kingdom.

━━◆━━

Repentance is the way to be saved. Believing is the way to be saved. Confessing is the way to be saved. But to qualify for service in the kingdom, we must be found faithful.

Some who expect to be part of the kingdom of heaven will not make it:

> *Many will say to me in that day, Lord, Lord, have we not prophesied in thy name? and in thy name have cast out devils? and in thy name done many wonderful works?*
>
> Matthew 7:22

"Many"! Clearly some type of work is being done in these cases, but God has a very different viewpoint than does man. We always think that the race will go to the swift, but He sees things differently.

Some strive, but not *"lawfully"*:

> *And if a man also strive for masteries, yet is he not crowned, except he strive lawfully.*
>
> 2 Timothy 2:5

There is a working that is not approved by the Lord, a striving upon which He cannot place His seal. There are apparent winners of the race who get where they are some other way. These are quickly and decisively disqualified:

> *I never knew you; depart from Me, you who practice lawlessness.*
>
> Matthew 7:23 NAS

"I never knew you." How powerful! Working outside the law is not an option we want to consider when it comes to matters of the kingdom. This is God's kingdom, and it must be operated in His way. And, since He is truth and light, the deeds of His kingdom must be done in truth and in light.

The next verse of Matthew begins with that telling word *therefore.* Jesus declared that He would not know some although they have purported to work miracles and do many good deeds. We are about to learn the *"therefore"* of that statement:

> *Therefore whosoever heareth these sayings of mine, and doeth them, I will liken him unto a wise man, which built his house upon a rock.*
>
> Matthew 7:24

Those who build upon the rock will stand, and who are they? *"Whosoever heareth these sayings of mine, and doeth them."* What will be the result?

> *And the rain descended, and the floods came, and the winds blew, and beat upon that house; and it fell not: for it was founded upon a rock.*
>
> Matthew 7:25

The Rock, of course, upon which we are to build everything and to be ourselves built, is Jesus. Ignore His teachings at your own peril. All else is sinking sand, but this foundation is solid and enduring.

We Are Ordained to Bring Forth Fruit

God has ordained you that you should go and bring forth fruit:

> *Ye have not chosen me, but I have chosen you, and ordained you, that ye should go and bring forth fruit, and that your fruit should remain: that whatsoever ye shall ask of the Father in my name, he may give it you.*
>
> John 15:16

Becoming the Expression of the Father

He has saved you and gifted you for a purpose—that you might take what is His and invest it by touching the lives of others. He has ordained a harvest. Bring it forth.

In the end, you will hear those precious words: *"Well done, thou good and faithful servant: thou hast been faithful over a few things, I will make thee ruler over many things: enter thou into the joy of thy lord"* (Matthew 25:21). In that moment you will know that you have successfully become the expression of the Father in the earth.

THE CONCLUSION

Shine Where You Are Planted

The power of the smallest light must never be underestimated. A very tiny one once saved the lives of our entire family.

It was during the time we were living on the houseboat along the mighty Amazon, the mightiest river in the world. At its mouth, on the east coast of South America, the river spread out a yawning two hundred miles before emptying into the Atlantic Ocean. Thousands of miles upstream where we were evangelizing along its banks, the Amazon still ranged from one to three miles across, and it roared along with such force that it tore loose land and trees along its banks and carried them away. The best of swimmers could not survive its currents.

One night we had moored along the banks of the river in what seemed relatively gentle water, but that day it rained upstream, and during the night the river rose precipitously. As we slept, the water pulled at the houseboat until the moorings came loose, and we were set adrift. I awakened to discover that our lives were in peril.

Becoming the Expression of the Father

We were in total darkness and had already drifted far enough from the shore that no light could be seen to give me any point of reference. This produced in us a severe disorientation that only people who have been in a similar situation can understand.

The boat was equipped with a powerful spotlight that could reach out for half a mile, but that night its great beam was insufficient to illuminate the shoreline. I was not sure what I should do. Since there was no way I could determine proper direction, and since the anchor of the boat could not hold us in place, we were being helplessly swept along. We had to do something.

I started the engines knowing that I should at least rev them up enough to hold us against the current, but that done, I was unable to determine which direction we were going. We seemed to be moving in every direction at once.

The danger was that any minute the boat could be slammed into one of the many hardwood tree trunks that floated with the swift currents of the river, and then the hull would be damaged and spring a leak. We could even be sunk. What could we do? We seemed to be powerless to do anything to help ourselves at the moment, and we could only pray. That was the right thing to do.

The occupants of a small hut that stood near where the houseboat had been moored were awakened by the sound of the boat's engines. Realizing what our situation was and how dangerous it could be, the man of the house got out of bed, lit a small candle, and stood with it on the shore.

The light from that candle was certainly not enough to reveal the boat, but, as it turned out, that was not his purpose. Instead, I was able to see the faint light from the candle flickering far in the distance (we were nearly a mile away by this time), and that is what the man had intended. That little light provided me with an orientation, with the direction I needed to head the boat back to safety. That night a tiny candle saved us all from certain damage and possible death.

The Conclusion

Don't be so much concerned about the size of your lamp. Even the smallest one can save lives. Just let yours shine. God has placed you in your own firmament for that purpose.

There may be other lights that are greater than yours, but they may not be in the right place at the right time. If that wonderful spotlight that was in the boat had been on the shore that night, it could have served as the candle did. But it wasn't there; only the candle was. The light from the candle wasn't much, but it was enough. Shine where God has placed you. Dare to be the expression of the Father in your world, and see what God will do for you and for those around you.

ABOUT THE AUTHOR

Charles A. Haun was a pastor, evangelist, missionary, Bible school teacher, and author. Born in 1929, Charles attended Robert Morris Business School, served in the United States Air Force, and then graduated from Eastern Bible Institute in Greenlane, Pennsylvania, in 1957. After serving as a pastor, Rev. Haun was a missionary in Iquitos, Peru, to the headhunters of the Amazon headwaters for over ten years. In 1972 Charles began a professorship at Western Pennsylvania Bible Institute in Butler, Pennsylvania. In 1978 Charles fulfilled God's leading to Israel. There in Jerusalem he taught the Bible and studied Hebrew. After returning to the United States in 1980, he made his home in Altamonte Springs, Florida. He traveled the United States and many foreign countries bringing richness from the Word not readily found. Charles and his wife Violet have four daughters, Telva, Renay, Brenda, and Cynthia, and ten grandchildren.

You can visit his ministry's website at
www.TeachingAllNations.com.